Coon Hunting In
Schuyler County, Illinois

Coon Hunting In
Schuyler County, Illinois

DON LERCH

iUniverse, Inc.
Bloomington

Coon Hunting In Schuyler County, Illinois

iUniverse books may be ordered through booksellers or by contacting:

iUniverse
1663 Liberty Drive
Bloomington, IN 47403
www.iuniverse.com
1-800-Authors (1-800-288-4677)

Because of the dynamic nature of the Internet, any web addresses or links contained in this book may have changed since publication and may no longer be valid. The views expressed in this work are solely those of the author and do not necessarily reflect the views of the publisher, and the publisher hereby disclaims any responsibility for them.

Any people depicted in stock imagery provided by Thinkstock are models, and such images are being used for illustrative purposes only.
Certain stock imagery © Thinkstock.

ISBN: 978-1-4759-4367-2 (sc)
ISBN: 978-1-4759-4368-9 (hc)
ISBN: 978-1-4759-4369-6 (ebk)

Printed in the United States of America

iUniverse rev. date: 09/06/2012

I WOULD LIKE TO DEDICATE THIS BOOK TO

MY WIFE CHAR OF 42 YEARS AND MY

FRIEND JACKIE GODDARD FOR HER WORK

SHE HAS DONE TO HELP MAKE THIS BOOK

POSSIBLE

This book is meant to honor present and past coon hunters

Coon hunting is like Country Music it is here to stay

Thank You to everyone who wrote a story.

I have lived in Schuyler County all my life. I have had a lot of things happen my sixty-nine years. I have been run off the road by other drivers, done things in my teenage years that people go to jail for today.

I also coon hunted from the time I was a young boy till I was not able to. I've been lost many a night, ran out of gas while hunting on the river but we always went back the next night. When buying fur some people did not know one animal from another as you will read in a story, in this book wrote by a friend who also bought fur. If you have hunted at all you should enjoy this book, there are many interesting stories to be read. I have had a lot happen over the years. As time passes things do change. When I was a child hunting coons and selling fur, for some families it was their means for survival. Many families lived on wild game through the winter because it was all they had. You will read about all of this in the stories to follow written by past and present hunters.

I was born in Oakland Township in 1943 at the True Dodge farm which is now owned by Ed Jones family. I am the seventh child of Marion (Mike) and Margaret Lerch. Bob was the oldest, then Walter, Mary Margaret, Marion (Bert), Carl, Betty, Don, Jack, Larry & Joan.

We moved from the Dodge place to the Scripps place on the Scotts Mill Road where I started school at. Dad bought a farm in Woodstock Township. It was a seventy nine acre farm, which is not very big compared to today. I went to school all eight years at Bethel School. It was a two room building, grades one through four was taught by Lena Elliott and grades five through eight were taught by Hazel Shields. We lived just east of Ripley at the time I started to coon hunt. I was eight years old. We didn't have reliable transportation at that time, so we hunted a lot around home. One night on a coon hunt along Crooked Creek with our two hounds, Blue & Buck they hit on a mink scent. They really got confused because the mink went from tree top to tree top.

One night we went to Industry to the Windmill Restaurant and meet Carl Lashbrook to go hunting. In those days you had to come to Rushville and go out the Old Macomb Road to get to Industry. As a young boy I felt like we had traveled a hundred miles, but we killed five coons that night.

On another night it was snowing pretty hard but I kept after Dad to go hunting, and he finally gave in and we took off walking behind our house, after about thirty minutes of tracking, the dogs came to a tree and sat at the bottom of it looking up and treeing. We looked the tree over because we knew this was a den tree, but we didn't expect what we saw next. A big coon was sitting on the outside of the hole, in those days coon hunters used a shotgun and Dad shot the coon out of the tree. Dad said "there he is" and started walking back to the house, leaving me to carry the coon. When we got home we weighed him and he weighed thirty-two pounds.

As I got older I spent a lot of time in Ripley with my good friend David Hendricks who we called "Digger". When Ripley had its homecoming celebration, Digger and I would go squirrel hunting in the morning and pitch horseshoes in the afternoon. The Ripley homecoming was a big event in those days, the food was provided by the church ladies, served by the men. I can still see Roger Vincent serving food. There were carnival rides for the kids and music for the adults way into the night. I remember Russell Trone and my brother Bob playing music.

Now back to coon hunting. Dad always stretched the hides on a board with a pointed end for the head of the coon, then put them in the shed to dry before they would be able to be sold to a man named John Spates a fur buyer whose business was operated from a building that is next to Ted's Barber Shop. One winter when dad got ready to take the hides to town, he went to the shed to get them and they were all gone, someone had stolen all of our coon hides. Dad thought he knew who had them, but he never did tell me. One day our dog came home real sick, so we took him to Dr Scott the vet. He was in the building where Simpson had his dry cleaning business. The Dr looked the dog over and said that he had been fed poison or ground glass in liver. As far as I know dad never owned another dog after that. When we lived in the country, mom used an old fashion cook stove to cook our meals, she would take a young coon remove all the fat and bake it in the oven with potatoes all around it until it was about half done then she would fry it until it was very tender, it made a very good meal. My mother and aunt Caroline always made coon dressing for Ernie Utters wild game feed that he had at least once a year at Rattlesnake Ranch, and it always tasted better outdoors at a place like that and so did the coon dressing. When we moved to town in 1960, I worked for Les Gains on a farm just east of Ripley. I didn't have a car, so Les let me drive his 1950 Studebaker pickup truck. At that time you were hired by the week, my weekly pay was thirty dollars. One morning when I was driving to work in the old Studebaker truck just past Scripps Park at the curve, a car ran me off the road and I turned the truck over and the car never stopped. Les came out there and he was not very happy, I think he didn't believe my story, luckily R.G. Smith was driving right behind the car and seen everything. He told Less what had happened and everything was alright.

While we were moving to town dad sold our seventy nine acres and let the equipment go with it for nine thousand dollars. He had sold five acres across the road prior to this sale. He bought a house in town for six thousand dollars at 400 Silverleaf. Dad worked at the old high school. He and Bill Trone cut and sold firewood for extra income. One day while dad was at work Bill went to the woods alone at the Lawrence Hollenbeck farm, he had cut through a tree but it never fell. Bill set the saw down and at that moment a breeze came up and blew the tree down right on top of the saw breaking it into little pieces.

I didn't hunt for about three years because I didn't have a car or any money. Les said I needed a car and we would work something out. He took me to a junk yard near Macomb we found a 1950 Ford with the front end wrecked. The owner of the junkyard said he would take the front end of another car and put it on this one, and then they painted the whole car blue and it was really nice. Les made the deal for $250.00 and took so much a week out of my $30.00 pay till it was paid. Les was good to do this for me.

After I quit working for Les, I worked part time for Larry Paisley at his Mobile station and part time for Charlie Burnside which I later owned. Between the two I made $40.00 a week. I traded my Ford for a 1953 Buick.

One July day while the fair was going on some gals stopped at the station when I went to the fair that night they were there. I was playing a game and won a teddy bear, the gals were behind me and I gave the bear to one of the gals, even though I didn't know her name. Later I found out that her name was, Charlene but everyone called her "Char". We started seeing each other and dated for about two years. During that time I went to work for Charlie "Doc" Barrett at the S & B oil station on the old Macomb Road. After I worked there for a while I traded for a 1956 Ford. When I was working for S & B other workers were Howard Trone, Squire Harris, and even Larry Paisley helped some. Doc Barrett was one of the best people I have ever known. When Char and I were married in September of 1963, Doc raised my wages to $60.00 a week.

We started out living in a 8 x 36 house trailer and later traded it for a 12x 60.

When Doc took over the Enco bulk truck he had to find someone to run the station at the corner of Liberty & Adams so he ask me if I would like to be on my own, he said he would set me up. The equipment was $800.00 and Doc loaned me the money. I had $50.13 when I started in 1964. Doc put in the gas from the bulk truck, I sold it then paid him for it. Addie Rebman owned Rushville auto parts, he would let me have parts and pay for them later, Bud Rice at Rice's garage would help me if I got a job I didn't understand, he always knew what to do, these people really helped me get my start.

Char and I were married for 42 years, we adopted 2 children, Dawn & Charles. Dawn has 3 children, Skyler, Shelby and & Madison. Charles has 4 children Chase, Charlee, Hannah & Emily. Now that I am older and think back to my younger days I wonder how I lived through it. My friends and I would ride around and drink beer before we were of age. I remember drag racing down the main street in Rushville, things you would be arrested for today.

Back to coon hunting, I started to hunt again in 1964, Digger Hendricks gave me a black & tan pup and I started to hunt with Dick Bowers and Jim Henninger. When Mr. Spates retired from his store there was a demand for a fur buyer in Rushville, so I decided to try it. That made coon hunting more fun. At that time a coon hide was either good or bad. A good one was worth $1.00 or $2.00 and a bad one was worth .25 or .50 cents. We would put on night hunts. Each hunter would pay $2.00 to enter. At the end of the hunt the money was split between the three hunters, the one with the heaviest, the one with the lightest, and we would draw a lucky number from a hat.

After a year or two Dick Powell, Dick Chockley and Dick Bower and I decided to start a Schuyler County Coon Hunting Club, membership dues were $5.00 per family. There was a feed each fall for all members at Rattlesnake Ranch. At one time we had over 120 members, we even had a judge and lawyer members who didn't even hunt. The second year we elected officers and a board that set up bylaws. We would either have the hunts at my business or Vic's feed store in Camden. The club would run a food stand at the Schuyler County Fair to raise money. We finally got a club house that Wayne Morrell made happen because he didn't charge what it was worth, at one time it was a church. Wayne had a son-in-law that was a coon hunter, and he did a lot of work to improve the building as most members did. The club is still going today. As a fur buyer everyone thought I was getting rich. Most years I made $1000.00 to $1500.00 dollars. One year on opening night of coon hunting the price of hides was $20.00 and no one could believe it. We would buy a pickup truck load a week with a topper on the truck. If we gave $20.00 each, by the time we sold them each hide would go up $5.00 each. This went on all season. The price went up to $60.00. The construction workers wanted to get laid off so they could hunt and draw unemployment. When coons were cheap and you got 2 or 3 treed you would pick out the big one and leave the other two. But when they were high priced most hunters would take them all. Most everyone got a dog. We sold traps, lights, knives and dog food for about two years. We could not keep enough supplies in stock.

The ones that didn't have a dog bought live traps, we ordered them by the truck loads. When Dick Bowers and I was out hunting one night I remember telling him that I made more money selling supplies in 3 months than my dad made in 1 year, I made $10,000.00 dollars that year by just selling supplies and furs. The higher price of fur made it harder to buy from some hunters. I remember a person came in with a hundred or more hides and I gave him a bid which he turned down. Later his dad told me he got .10 cents a hide more but it had cost him $20.00 in gas to do it. It was good while it lasted, but when it became more about the money and less about the sport coon hunting was almost ruined, you could not even give supplies away as it turned out I did give some away, as I was never paid for them. There is still some coon hunting, but not as much as there was "in the old days". We had 2 deer hunting seasons of 3 days each out of all the coon season. Today we have deer season of some kind all winter long and farmers have leased their land to the deer hunters and it makes it hard to hunt if you don't own your own ground. When I hunted the farmers would ask you to come hunt because most of them raised hogs and the coons would eat the hog feed. One day I was talking to Don Aten, he said he had sold a lot full of hogs, it was spring time and the windows were open in the house that night and in the middle of the night he heard the feeder lids banging up and down. He thought he had missed getting all the pigs, it turned out it was the coons in the feeders he said they emptied the feeder as fast as the hogs did. My dog digger turned out to be a pet for about the first 2 years. Dick and Jim had trained dogs, and Dick had a dog named "Buzz" and Jims dog was named "Moon". They were both good coon dogs. When we went hunting and I sat down, Digger sat down. We even put him in a barrel with a live coon and it didn't help. I took him every time we went hunting the next year. On the first hunt of the third year the dogs hit a track and low and behold there was a third voice! Digger was running a coon, and from that night on he ran coons like he had been doing it all his life. But one morning I got up and I discovered Digger was gone, he had dug out of his pen. At that time we lived on the dump road north of the fairgrounds, our friend Dale Smith came to the station that day and wanted to know if I was missing a dog and I told him I was. He told me he was going home the night before when a coon had ran out in front of him and right behind the coon was a dog, he tried to swerve to miss the dog but could not. I want out to check and it was my dog Digger.

One day I was working at the station and Barb Phillips pulled up in her 1958 Thunderbird, she said she had picked up a coon on the way to town and wanted to sell it. As we raised the lid of the trunk, the coon raised straight up! I grabbed a tire iron and killed it. After my dog Digger got ran over I got a blue tick pup from Lee Herche, and named him "Lee" because that was the way dogs were names a lot of the times, by where you got the dog. Jim Henninger named his dog "Moon" because he got him from Moon Busby and Dick Bowers named his dog "Buzz" because he got his from one of the Busby's. The first season of coon hunting, Lee was doing real well running coons and treeing a little when he got sick with some kind of bowel trouble. I took him to the vet, Dr. Wilson. We tried 4 or 5 different kinds of food, vitamins, and shots but nothing helped. After spending four of five hundred dollars, which I could not afford that time, he died. It was only the beginning of his second season of coon hunting. My next dog was another blue tick from near Quincy. I named him "Blue". After I got Blue, one night I went on a hunt with Don Fagan and Jr. Utter. We went up north to the Moore farm, it was a nice night when we started. The dogs had treed 3 or 4 coons when the fog had started to roll in. The dogs kept on running and treeing coons and we got lost in the fog. We walked and walked and still were lost, we finally realized we had seen the same fence post 3 times and knew we had been walking in circles. We could hear the big trucks on Hwy 67, so we followed the sound until we got to a gravel road and found our truck. Jr Utter was older than me, but I could not keep up with him. He could skin a coon and never quit walking and that is no joke.

One night Dick Bowers, Jim Henninger and I went to the Beardstown Bay to put the boat in the water, we would shine the banks with a spot light until we spotted a coon eating along the bank, then we would run the boat over to where the coon was and let the dogs out on a hot trail, this was a good was to train dogs, but not legal. When we left Beardstown we had the boat tank was full and we took five gallons of gas a quart of oil with us. Our plan was to go until we ran out of gas and oil then put the extra gas and oil in to get back. Everything was going fine, we were getting coons then we ran out of gas. So when we ran out of gas Dick picked up the gas can and put the extra gas in and ask for the oil, Jim looked at me and I looked at him, we had left the oil in the truck in Beardstown! Why we didn't mix it before I don't know. Dick stood up and said "My God boys we are close to Nap Island". So we started off down stream. When a barge would come along we would get over to the bank and hold on to the boat until it passed. We would paddle awhile and float awhile. Every time we would see a boat tied up we would check to see if they had any oil. No luck we checked 4 or 5 boats. We walked over to the levee and saw a house, Jim knocked but could not raise anyone, then Dick went to knock and looked down and saw a qt of oil not quite full, we took the oil and walked back over the levee added the oil to the gas and headed home. It was almost daylight, our wives were quite upset, but happy to see us. We found out later that where we got the oil was Gobels pump house, Jim said he was going to send them $2.00 but I don't know if he ever did.

One night I was at John Ingles Grill and pool room on the east side of the square when Jr Utter came in and said "lets go hunting", and I said "you've got to be kidding" as there was about 5 inches of snow on the ground, and it was cold. I said "do you have your dogs?" he said "they are in their box in the back of my truck". It was around 8:00 pm. Everyone in the place thought we were nuts including myself, but away we went east of town on the sale barn road. Just after Don Atens house was a small draw and a hog lot on the other side. I told Jr. to pull in here and we would hunt in the draw. We let his dogs out and in a few minutes they started to "Boo hoo". Now and then after a awhile we could hear them and then we couldn't. The draw was only about a quarter of a mile long, so we walked up the draw and found the dogs had treed in the ground. Jr said "we wont get them coons out". So it was about 9:00 pm, I walked up to Atens house to get a spade. I knocked on the door. Don came to the door and I told him what I wanted and why. He let me have a spade and I took it down to where I had left Jr. The dogs had been digging in the hole where they had located the coon. We dug 2 nice coons out and went back to the pool hall to show everyone what we had done, the guys couldn't believe it, but it really happened.

One night Dick Powell and I went hunting on the Jr Moore farm north of Rushville right off Rt 67. We had treed a coon or two. The dogs were running a track then they would stop for a awhile and then run again. After doing this for awhile they tried to tree, just running back and forth, when we got close to where they were we saw a sow and a litter of piglets close to the tree. We got a little closer and here came the sow after us. It wasn't very funny at the time, because she meant business! We found out later that there were lots of sows with piglets in the woods. When it was over Dick would tell that story over and over and laugh, he would say "I didn't know Lerch could move that fast"! Back

when we sold hunting and fishing license a fishing license was $2.25 and a hunting license was $3.25 and we got to keep .25 cents of each one we sold. Later fishing license was raised to $5.50 and we got to keep .50 cents. You were allowed 50 hooks per license. The hunting license cover most all hunting except deer, which required a special permit also you didn't have to buy a fur stamp, that came later. One good thing about selling the license was we didn't have to pay for them until they were sold. At the end of the month and at the end of the year we would send back whatever we had not sold and pay the balance.

One day Bryon Bartlow was in the station getting some work done on his pickup truck, and he mentioned he'd like to go do some coon hunting. A few nights later was a nice winter night and Bud Rice wanted to go. So that night Dick Bowers, Bud and his little boy Scott and I went by and picked up Bryon and headed out north of town which at that time was owned by the coal mine. We were doing real well, we had killed and skinned 6 coons by nine o'clock. Then the wind came up and we could no longer hear the dogs and we knew we were lost. We walked till Scott got tired, so we took turns carrying him. We finally found the truck after about 3 or 4 hours and everyone was worn out, then we had to wait another hour or so for the dogs and then we started home. We dropped Bryon off at his house about 3:00 am and still just had 6 coons. As we let him out Bryon said "Next time you go hunting, don't call me . . . I'll call you" he never called us again!!

A lot of nights after a hunt we would agree that we should rest the next night, but when the sun started to go down, I would start thinking about hunting and I would be calling someone or they would be calling me. We would be making plans about where we would go, and pretty soon one would be picking up the other and we would be hunting another night. You didn't have to be crazy but it helped.

One night Dick and Jim couldn't go so I called Dick Powell, when he came and picked me up he had Breeze Mitchell with him. We went out by Park Shields farm and parked down by the church. We went north from the road where the people in the past use to dig coal by hand. We were having trouble treeing up the tree rather than holes in the ground. We decided to go somewhere else and try it. Going back up the road to the truck here came Powells dog which we caught and put on a leash, then my dog, I had left my leash in the truck so I said "Breeze loan me your leash" which he did, then came Breezes dog. He caught it but didn't have a leash because I had his and he said "Lerch, why don't you get your own leash, you have a store full of them" I said "I don't see anything wrong with the one I have". He didn't think that was very funny, but he got over it. We moved on down the road and let the dogs loose and had a good hunt.

Jim Henninger couldn't go with us every night because he raised a lot of hogs. They were always having little ones during coon season. At that time he would stay in the hog houses all night if he had to. When he could go, he would stay in the woods all night if anyone else would, but on nights when we had to work the next day 1 or 2 o'clock was way to late, most of the time we tried to be home by midnight, if the weather was real bad we would stay home and rest.

One Thanksgiving morning I got up in terrible pain. I went to see Dr Dohner and he said I would probably pass a kidney stone, we were going to Chars parents that day for dinner and I told Char I need to stay home and rest, but that night at dark I was ready to go hunting.

In the 70's Dick Powell had a dog named "Rambler". The name on his papers was "Nick" but he was called Rambler. His sires full name was "Smokey River Blue Rambler". Powell had the dog for sale at that time for $1000.00. At that time hides were $2.00. This dog was one of the best and Dick Powell was one of the best trainers I have ever known. He trained coon or rabbit or whatever kind, he was the best. I wanted Rambler but I could not afford to buy him. So Dick Bowers and I went together and bought the dog each paying half, everyone thought we were crazy, including my wife!. One good thing about it, our wives were good friends. They would often visit while we were out hunting, sometimes they would both be asleep when we came back.

One night Jim Henninger went with us north of town on a hunt, we had a good hunt and killed a few coons. Rather than carry the whole coon back, we skinned them in the field. The car was parked in a clover field, the dogs started to run a track and treed it at the clover field. Dick and Jim went to the tree and I went to get the car, on the way I heard a shot, then the dogs fighting the coon. I could hear them talking, I got to the car and heard them talking. I heard Dick ask Jim where he was going, Jim said "I'm going to the car" and Dick said "your going the wrong way-that's toward Littleton" Dick yelled for me to honk the horn, so I did. In about five minutes they were at the car, Jim got in to drive, hit his hand on the steering wheel and said "I know I was wrong but I think I was right" After we got Rambler we aimed to get 100 coons a year, which we did, except for the last year with him when coon were high priced.

Dick and I left a truck at Clipper Crossing and gone to Ray in another truck to walk the railroad tracks back to Clipper Crossing. It was easy walking and now and then we would get a coon. Then all of the sudden Rambler treed, then before we got there we heard a shot and Rambler quit treeing. As we walked around the corner, we could see truck lights going the same way we were down the tracks. They were shinning both sides of the tracks, getting coons any way they could. After that the night hunt was not so good. When we got to Clipper Crossing, we could see the truck sitting there and just behind it was the game warden. We found out later the men were from Vermont and they were given some tickets and we lost a coon or two.

The second year we owned Rambler the price of coons went as high as $60.00, so we more than paid for Rambler. Sometime around 1977 we started raising pups and selling them, we had a female named Brandy. You can tell at a young age which pups will make good hunting dogs and the ones that will not be so good.

Jim Henninger, Ed Skiles and I went hunting one night, the dogs were running a coon in a standing corn field, they would leave the corn field, go over the hill, mark the tree, then the coon would start up the tree go back down and right back to the corn field. We sat there and talked for awhile and then Ed said "I am going to see what's going on" Ed was standing by the tree and here came the coons, one tried to climb up him, you should have seen Ed jump up and down!! After that the dogs lost their track and it ended a very good coon chase.

One night Dick and I went hunting at Clipper Crossing, it was a frosty night, not a real good night to hunt and we hadn't had any luck at all. Rambler came to us, so we put him on a leash and started up the road to the truck. About half way up, Rambler let out a bark so we turned him loose. He ran up over a bank and treed. We shot the coon and I was reminded of the old days with my dad. When we weighed the coon it was 32 lbs the same as the one I had shot with my dad all those years ago. After that Rambler got sick. We took him to two different vets who couldn't find anything wrong. Dr Bob Goodin a vet in Virginia at the time sent us to an animal research center at the U of I in Champaign. They said there were crystals in the bloodstream and the only thing that might cause that was if the dog had eaten frozen rhubarb tops or drank anti-freeze. Rambler could not tree a coon after that, he would try and try but could not do it. Rambler lived a year or two after that. When he quit I guess I quit too. He was the best dog I ever owned.

About 1979 Char and I decided to do away with the gas station, after all we still sold boats, bait and tackle, hunting supplies and bought furs plus an ice route. David Bowman delivered ice and dog food for many years. I had called Dick Powell and said I wanted to have an auction, he didn't believe me, so he came to town and we set a date for the auction, then there was a lot of work to be done, cleaning things up and display it for the sale. The tires and batteries were marked with list pricing. The auction went great, some things brought more than we sold them for, one set of rear tires I had priced to a farmer, put on and he didn't buy them and came to the sale and paid more for them and I didn't have to put them on. The auctioneers did a great job.

When we had the station we also had a bait and tackle shop in a twenty by forty building east of the station. When Schuy-Rush park opened ever Friday evening and Saturday our drive would be full of people buying bait and tackle. My dad Mike ran the bait shop and he would also run and get parts and such for the station. Dad got a percent of what we sold, in the summer that was real good for someone retired. After dad passed away and we had no one to run the bait shop, my uncle Fritz retired from Green Motors as parts man which he had done for years, I gave him the same deal as dad. I put pool tables and games in the station part for a short time. One evening Chuck Clayton came in the game room where we had seating for people, it was full of older guys. Chuck had been in a week or so earlier and needed to cash a check but didn't have one with him so I said "how much cash do you need" he said "fifty dollars" and I gave it to him. The next time he was in town he brought me a check, wanted to cash it for $100.00 to repay me an have an extra $50.00. The seats were full of guys again, so I cashed Chucks check and I gave him $50.00 of the $100.00 dollars and told him I would give him the other $50.00 when the check cleared the bank, he called me names and left, you could have heard a pin drop and no one ever said a word. We ran our business this way for awhile then Don Fagan wanted to sell his food store business, which also carries package liquor. It took about thirty days to come together on a price, finally I said I would take it if the city would give me a license. Don and I went to the next city meeting, Bob McMillian was mayor at the time he told the other members what we were there for and they all agreed to give me a license. When I got my license in 1980 you had to buy another business to have a license because there were just to many license. That amount went by population of the city. When L.D. Smith was mayor he started giving out more license. If I could have walked in and asked for a license like the rest of them did I could have saved fifteen thousand dollars or more. It is worse today as far as license.

Before I could move Fagan's store to mine I had to build a room on. Fagans store was known as Fords food store and now it is where the Rushville Vet Clinic is now. I did not buy the food permit or building. Fagan sold out the food and sold the building to Dr Lunt. Dick Sowers built a room on the west side of my business, we could only build so far because you had to stay one hundred feet from building to building from a church. If you look around town some don't look to be one hundred feet. So we did ours right and I guess that was the main thing. After we had our building done and all our license which was state, federal, city and sales tax numbers which we already had. One Sunday we got help and started to move coolers and product from Fagans store to ours. We had a lot of help. Freddie Jones had a load on his truck and said it was worth more than his truck! It took about a week before we opened. David Bowman helped us at that time. Between David, myself and my wife Char it opened in a week for business. Soon after we opened the liquor store we got some evening help three or four night a week. Our first help was Frank Ford and my sister Betty. Frank had worked in stores before and Betty had work in restaurants and knew a lot of the public. They both were an asset to our business. After we went into the liquor business we quit buying furs in 1980. I found out later my mother Margaret was not happy about our purchase of a liquor business or that Betty was working there. After we opened the liquor store we began to do away with other things. I think the pool tables was the first and then the bait and tackle shop, because Uncle Fritz got to where he couldn't do it and I could not run two businesses at once. We also made ice and had a route in Rushville, Camden, Coal Mine, Mt Sterling, Industry, Astoria & Browning. Crystal Ice from Iowa kept trying to buy my ice business and I didn't think it was enough. Each year their offer would be more, about the third year our equipment was getting old and they offered an amount that was a good price, so I sold. After that we bought our ice from them. At one time on the fourth of July and the Schuyler County Fair was going on we could not keep up with ice. Schwans would even let us store some at their plant, we would have Budweiser bring over their beer trailer with an extra three hundred cases of beer in it and sold all of it. At that time a case of Budweiser was around ten dollars. Times have changed!! When the fair was in town it helped every business, not so much any more. The fair buys and sells the ice and also has a beer tent, you cant blame them, the way times are today they need every penny they can get just to be able to have a County fair. After we had done away with everything except the liquor store, my brother-in-law John Bowman knocked a wall out in between the two rooms and doubled the size of our store, my brothers Bob and Larry would help fill the coolers at times and do other things that needed to be done. They would never take any money so Char and I would buy them lunch whenever we could. Brother Bert and Larry painted the building one time and I had trouble getting them to take anything but I made them take it. Later Bob worked one day a week which I paid him for it. One day Merlin Southerland came into the store, he worked for the Illinois State Lottery and wanted to know if I wanted to sell lotto tickets. Merlin also said he had asked others before he thought of us and no one wanted to sell them. I said let me think about it for a few days. When he came back we had decided to do it. Frank Ford and my sister Betty were still helping and we all had to go to Springfield for training. Char, Betty, Frank and myself went and on the way home Frank said "you have gotten us into a lot, but this is the worst"! Selling lotto tickets was a good thing for us, we made 5% for selling tickets and 1% on all winnings over one thousand dollars. We sold a million dollar winner, seven little lotto winners and two second place winners on the big game. It was always funny to me when someone would buy five dollars worth of instant and win two dollars and I would ask them "do you want the two dollars or two more tickets" and some would say "I'll take the two dollars and quit while I'm ahead!" To me that was three dollars behind not two dollars ahead! We would always play tricks back and forth, one morning some guys were playing instant tickets and Freddie Jones played some and didn't win, Dick Powell said Lerch give me a couple of them" Dick rubbed them off and said "I don't believe it ", and handed me the tickets and I said "you won a hundred dollars" and I gave Dick a hundred dollars, you should have heard Freddie!! Dick really had not won and after Freddie left Dick gave me the money back. One of the best days we ever had was New Years Eve 1999 Jackie Goddard was helping and all she got done was to keep putting product in the coolers. It was sold before it ever got cold but no one cared, they would just buy ice. Jackie, Char myself and someone else (I can't remember who) sold eight thousand dollars worth of product that day, plus lotto tickets. The worst thing was trying to keep things dust free. Char and I or someone else dusted the whole place at least once a month. There were a lot of people throughout the years that helped us dust. Jackie Goddard and Sue Carey were part time help, they were both good workers, you never had to tell them what to do they would just do it. Sue worked for us until we retired. Between Char my wife and Sue they were my right hand. On December 5th 2005 we sold our store to Jim and Robin Bowers, and Sue still worked there when we sold out. On February 24th 2006 my wife Chad passed away, and nothing has been the same since. I do have a lot of friends and memories. I will stop for now so this won't get to boring. The stories from here on are from other coon hunters from the surrounding area. I hope you will enjoy this book as much as I have putting it together.

Don and his 32# coon in the 80's

WE WERE LOST

By Tony Allen

Have you ever had a night that you thought would never end? This was one of them.

My grandpa Gilbert and I went coon hunting and was not going to be gone long so we thought! We got to the field and let Ole Doc lose so far so good. We made it across the corn field and Doc treed a Coon. I bet we shot 50 or 60 shots before we figured out the rifle site was off. Ole Doc got tired of us shooting so he sat down and watched us. We finally shot the coon. So after skinning the coon we looked around and thought we were heading in the right direction, we followed the creek and came on some tracks, I said "Grandpa are them our tracks" and he said "no we haven't made it to the corner of the field yet". Ok so three hours later we stopped walking and grandpa just stopped and was looking at this tree and he didn't say a word, but I knew it was the same tree we shot the coon out of because of all the 22 shells around the tree. Meanwhile uncle Bud got worried and came looking for us and found us—thank God or we would still be there! We never found the forth corner because it was a three corner field, the creek wrapped around so our short night was a long and very interesting night and I would do it all over again if I could.

BEST GRANDPARENTS

By Tony Allen

Coon hunting was always a big deal in the Allen home and my Grandparents was all into it. It started out like any other night, dark and cold. The whole family was at Grandma and Grandpa's house. Grandma Julia always carried a lantern and hard candy. Grandpa Gilbert always packed his smokes, rifle and horehound candy.

Grandpa Gilbert was set on having Walker dogs, that is all we wanted. We were down by Hester's hunting the bottoms when old Jack and Doc treed a coon. We got to where the dogs had treed their prize, and the ole coon was looking down at us! Les, my brother and I watched as dad, Terry and Grandpa shot the coon out of the tree, the dogs got the coon and we skinned it.

The older ones were talking about crossing the branch and moving Jack and Doc on around the ben. We rolled up the hide and started out. Grandma was having a time with the brush and her lantern as we went to cross the branch. The ice and brush got the best of her and she fell. I tried to grab her, but I missed, Les missed as well. There she was on her back, plum soaked of course everyone thought it was funny. Grandpa said "mom if you can't stand you need to go home"! and then he no more got that out of his mouth and he said "we need to make sure she is ok" she said she was, all the time rolling his cigarette, and then he said "Well since I'm here I might as well finish rolling my smoke"! He never did lose any of his tobacco on his rolling paper. By the end of the night we had gotten 3 or 4 coons. Us boys got to eat a lot of hard candy. Not long before Grandpa died he would still smile about that hunt. I don't know if I loved to coon hunt or coon hunting with the Allen family, but us grandkids got to spend a lot of time in the woods with two of the best grandparents any grandkids could ask for!

THE MOUNTED COON

By Dick Bowers

One night Don Lerch and I was going to go coon hunting at my farm northwest of town. We called this farm Jacks place because an ole fellow by that name lived there. He had no where to live so I let him live there so no one would bother anything there. Don had a mounted coon that had seen better days. On the way to go coon hunting we took the mounted coon, put it along the road, which was Old Macomb Road. I told Don he would have to be careful or he would but it back, at that time Don was buying fur. We went on our hunt and did have a nice evening in the woods. Around 11:00 o'clock we were close to the truck and we decided to call it a night with a couple of coons. We headed back to town the same way we went. When we got to where we put the mounted coon, it was gone . . . someone had picked it up! I let Don out and went on home. When I got home their on my yard gate hung the mounted coon, what a laugh I had.

The next day Don's fur buyer was coming after a load of furs, after they loaded the furs, I slipped the mounted coon in the load of furs. The next time Bud was at Don's I said something about the mounted coon, he said it was sure funny when they unloaded the fur one of his workers wanted it so he just gave it to him. The mounted coon had a new home.

MY FIRST COON
By Morris Billingsley

When I was 13 years old I got my first coon. We were sitting in the house one night and I heard the dog barking down in the bottoms. He kept it up for a long time so I decided to go down and see what he had. I lit the lantern and got the rifle and went down to see. It turned out to be a coon, the first one I had ever seen. The dog kept fighting and it took three shots before I got him. I took him to Rushville the next day and got five dollars he was not skinned.

That got me to hunting a lot. One night Dan Norvell and I went hunting and got 20 coons. We skinned them whenever we got one. We got back at midnight. The most coons we got up one tree was three.

I got the largest coon in the 1971 FFA coon hunt and the smallest coon in 1972 FFA coon hunt, and in 1973 I got the smallest coon in the Schuyler County coon hunt. I don't remember what year I quit hunting.

COON HUNTING WITH MY DAD

By Donna Bartlett

My dad, Don Egbert, was an enthusiastic coon hunter. He hunted frequently with Dick Bowers. They hunted several areas in Schuyler County.

One cold December night in the early 1950's they planned to go hunting and I begged to go along. I was only 5 or 6 years old at the time. After several attempts to distract me from wanting to go along, Dad agreed to take me. The plan was to go close to home since the weather was cold. I suited up with cold gear and boots. After treeing several coons, and walking a fair distance, I was tired and wanted to go home. Since we were a fair distance from home, dad put me on his back with my feet in the hip pocket of his coveralls, and away we went towards home. Meanwhile, the dogs treed several coons. By the time we got home, I could not feel anything in my feet but pain. Dad took me into the kitchen and soaked my feet in luke warm water to get the feeling to return. I went to bed that night with painful feet but still enjoying the hunt. I never asked to go hunting in very cold weather again.

A COLD WINTER NIGHT COON HUNT

By Jerry Bartlett

My dad, Bill Bartlett, was an avid coon hunter in the late 50's but never owned a coon hound. Ralph Ward owned a good coon hound and was always looking for a companion for his hunts. This combination provided an opportunity for many good hunts for the two of them. I occasionally joined the hunt and to be honest, I was ready to go home long before they were.

Ralph had one limitation that he depended on dad to help him with. He easily lost his sense of direction in the dark particularly after the excitement of treeing a coon. Dad took particular delight in teasing him about this and it made a lively exchange. Dad had the advantage on the hunts because he always took Ralph hunting in the Hale Ridge neighborhood where dad was raised and dad knew the area well.

A COON HUNT IN THE DARK

By Jerry Bartlett

My father-in-law Donald Egbert, was a hunter, trapper and fisherman for most of his life. One of his favorites was coon hunting. Donald owned coon hounds for many years and hunted often in fair and foul weather. I became acquainted with Donald in the late 60's after becoming acquainted with his daughter. Coon hunting was not one of my favorites but I knew Donald was an experienced hunter and I thought I could learn from him although I was at a disadvantage because I could not see very well in the dark. One evening he organized a hunt which included me, his brother Glen and his other son-in-law Donnie Gragg. The night was cold and crisp which I was told was a perfect night. The negative for my part that night was the dark phase of the moon. Immediately after getting underway the dogs treed a coon and Donald dispatched it with one shot with his 22 pistol. After the coon was skinned I complained that I couldn't see well enough. After friendly criticism by the group for a period of time, Donald offered me the gas lantern to carry. I thanked him graciously and away we went the next coon. As we made our way through the woods, I gained confidence in my night vision and promptly stepped off a bank into waist deep water. I thought the laughter from the group would never end. Actually no harm was done except for my ego and my new work boots. That was my last coon hunt.

THE CHRISTMAS COON
By Ben Cain

Gary Ward, my neighbor and friend, and I was always coon hunting together. Coon prices were fairly high for the times. We had a real good dog, Kate, named after Gary's mother, and my dog, Edna May, named after Gary's aunt. Edna May was an excellent tracker and fighter until a coon bit one of her ears. After that she tracked, but left all the fighting to Kate.

All coons we got we kept in Gary's cellar until we were ready to sell them. Gary spread them out around the perimeter of the cellar and up the cellar stairs so they were easy to count. We had approximately 40 coons in his cellar. Gary always knew exactly how many, since he counted them at least every day. As he counted he would place his hand on each one to make sure his count was correct.

Coon hunting consumed a lot of our time since Gary which was usually ready at 6:00 pm and never quit before midnight. It did not matter if it was 5 below, raining or snowing, he still wanted to go and wouldn't take "no" for an answer from me. I had gotten to the point that I hated to hear the phone ring a little before 6:00 pm, because I knew he was on his way over to get me come hell or high water!

Late in November I got a phone call from Gary to come over to his house right away. When I got there he was very upset. He had counted the coons over and over. One coon was missing! He had me count them to see if I came up with the same count as his. I never paid that much attention to how many we had, so I thought what's one coon more or less. For the next month he speculated as to where the coon could have gone. I even began to wonder if he suspected that I had taken it.

On Christmas eve, Holly, Rob and I were invited to his mother-in-laws to join their families in opening gifts and eating supper. As soon as I walked in. I got a good cussing from Gary. There was the missing coon stuffed and perched on a log. His wife had snuck it out of the cellar and had it stuffed as a Christmas present for Gary. The grand theft had been solved.

Years after Gary and I had quit hunting, Gary's aunt and mother would want to know if their namesakes were behaving. Gary's son now has the coon at his house. It brings back good memories and makes me laugh every time I see it.

ONE HOUR HUNT

By John and Mike Carey

One night my son, Mike and I went coon hunting at the old place. We parked the ole truck up by the barn, and turned Babe, the ole blue tick loose. It was not very long and she picked up a track and was moving very fast. It was a hot track and in about twenty minutes Babe had treed a coon. We had our caps on with hunting lights, when we got to where ole Blue had treed we shined our light up the cotton wood tree. I started to see two eyes. I had a Smith & Wesson 22 pistol, so I shot one out. I shot again and got number two. The tree had limbs going every which way, so Mike was shining in all the limbs., he yelled "Dad there is one or two more over on this side." Mike got his gun and shot one and then the second one. That made four. Mike kept shining on the limbs, then I saw two old coons and three young ones all together. Not a bad haul for an hour hunt. This is a true story by John and Mike Carey. We also hunted many times in the FFA coon hunt. We got a couple trophies once since you didn't get anything else.

A FATHERS PRICELESS HUNT

By Lynn Carey

I was getting ready to go coon hunting one night when my son Matt said he wanted to go with me.

A little reluctant to take him with me because he was only around five or six years old. Always glad to take a kid hunting or fishing, I told him he could go, but he would have to walk and be able to keep up with me, cause I was not going to carry him. He said he would walk and he could keep up, so we were soon off to the woods. Living in the middle of Scab Hollow we were in some good but very rough walking for a little guy. It was a bad night for hunting, dry, cold and frost had already set in. After about an hour my old coon dog Brummy, a big female blue tick took off on a track and treed way down the holler. When we finally got there she had three coons treed up the same tree. I started shooting them out of the tree, and then Matt started yelling at me. He said "Dad, this is better than six flags aint it!. The look on his face was priceless, I am so glad I took him hunting with me that night. I will never forget that and I am sure he won't either.

COON HUNTING WITH LLOYD AND JR.

By George Clark

One night in the middle of winter, I don't remember when probably in the 70's Lloyd Reische called me and said "ya want to go coon hunting" I said "ya. It don't look to bad out, I will go with ya." Weather didn't make much difference to him. He would hunt every night and stay out all night. If you didn't make him go home. He said "I am going to meet Jr Utter down at Cooperstown". I don't know if we were on Colclasure or Chet Hendricks or somewhere around there and turned loose the dog. I didn't take a dog. Lloyd took a blue tick and Jr. had a couple of walker dogs . . . kind of mixed up dogs, but I tell he kept some pretty good dogs. We went off and the hills aren't to high but the hollers are deep. You start off walking and the next thing you know your off in a holler, then, zoom your are headed for the creek. Those guys could skin a coon on the run, but I would have to stop to skin my coon. We got four coons that night and I was just along for the ride. I can tell you those boys are ardent coon hunters. Lloyd brought me home and it might have been midnight or a little later. I asked Lloyd in for a bowl of ice cream. He said "ya, he could eat some." I tell ya I wouldn't want to try to fill him up on ice cream because he could eat more ice cream than any feller I ever saw. If you would have kept filling up his bowl, he would have just kept eating. We did have a good time and Lloyd was a very good man to be with. Lloyd was just a GOOD MAN! A good friend and an ardent coon hunter.

THE NIGHT I COULDN'T GET ACROSS THE DRAW

By George Clark

Max wanted a coon hound when he was about 7th or 8th grade. It was a blue tick. I wondered if she would be any good the way the kids babied her around. She turned out to be a good hound and we raised a few pups out of her. Most of the pups turned out good. She had at least 3 litters and boy they sold good. One time Charlie Koch owned the old Ivan Hetrick farm down the road. I had the kids and they couldn't stay out late coon hunting because they had school the next day. The dog was over a year old and she had been treeing her own coons and doing pretty good. I said "we will go down to the old Hetrick place and turn her loose and see how we get along". It was a nice night in November. We turned the dogs loose and maybe got one coon, which is all we wanted any how. We parked on the west side of the draw, that was north of the house and would come out on Crooked Creek. We were on the east side of the draw and we were down quite a ways from where the truck was setting. We got the coon and I said "its time to get you kids home". So I though we would cross the draw and come up the ridge and come up by the side of the house. I was leading the dog on a leash. We started to cross the draw, every time we came out on the same side of the draw we started from. I felt like a fool! I thought, well I got to get across that draw. We could see Lanning's lights and I knew where I was at but, with a lead on the dog and thru the brush, I could not get across that draw. I said "we will walk up this way and go around it", and that's what we had to do. I COULD NOT get across that draw. Like I say I knew the way we had to get to the truck. We had to go clear to the east side of the draw.

FUR BUSINESS
By George Clark

A few years ago when I was still running the apple store, I still had a few trees left and run the cider mill. Betty and I was out running around over the country. We stopped by ole Ed Bowers fur buying station. He lived over south of Greenville down by St Louis. I stopped at Ed's to talk to him about buying furs. He said "well I could use somebody up there, I use to have somebody up there by the name of Elz (Smoke) Flynn", he said "I will set you up". I told the old man, "well I don't know anything about buying furs". Ed said "we will teach you". He called his boy, young Ed. I went with him and he showed me a lot of things about buying furs. They bought a lot of furs. They bought a lot that was not skinned. They had a boy working for them that would skin out muskrats. He would skin 500 a day. When he reached 500 he would quit and some days he would be done by noon . . . . talking a mile a minute all the time he was skinning them. When I went down there he had 10,000 muskrat hides. The market had dropped on him and he was holding them. He told me if he could just make 10 cents a piece on them, he would sell. They done their own scraping. They had a big operation. They bought a lot of furs out of the Dakota's, Northern Iowa, and Minnesota. I tell ya some of the hides he was getting out of that area would knock your eyes out. Sometimes their would 40 lbs coons up there, and that is a big coon. Those are the kind you could stretch on an ironing board. The thing I was most impressed with, was behind his desk was the prettiest bear hide you ever saw. All the way around the bear hide was 2 inches of red velvet. It still had the skull on it. It was beautiful. I ask him what he would take for it, but he said it wasn't for sale, but if I wanted one he could get me one. I never did follow it up. You would have to have a taxidermist to do the head and tan it. It sure would look good on my wall. So I came home and started buying hides. I talked to him about every two weeks to see how the market was doing. Apple season was over when fur season came in. On weekends I would start a fire in the old apple store and people would come in. I bought quite a bit of fur. I never lost any money on it.

The fact t is I made some money, buy the time I loaded the old station wagon up and went to Ed's, with the time and gas involved I probably didn't make a whole lot, but I had a lot of fun. I had people come in on weekends and had quite a session. I would put a pot of coffee on. Chet Hendricks would stop by about every week. Chet done some trapping. He trapped near a road down by Scott Blentlinger's. One day he came by and he was mad. Someone had taken his coon out of his trap, skinned out his hide and put the carcass back in the trap. Lloyd Reische came by later that day, and I ask him if he knew anything about it and he said he didn't, but we sure got a good laugh out of it. Chet was madder than an ole wet hen. We never did find out who done it, and probably a good thing we never did.

One time I had a feller come in from up around Camden, can't think of his name. He said "are you buying coyote dogs? I said "well I don't know what are you talking about "coyote dogs"? "I buy coyotes" He had 6 of them. I swear he had skinned out terriers they were black and white. I told the feller "I don't know what I can do with them, but I will see what Bower will give me for them and I will give you everything I can get out of them. He left them with me and I left them on the wall because I know it would make a good conversation piece. Everyone that came in said "well where did you get the dogs"? That was fun. Dick Baker came in on Saturday afternoon, I had known Dick for years, him and Doc McCoy (my first father-in-law) and I went fox hunting a few times together. Dick knew where every fox crossed. Dick looked at me and he said "GEORGE, WHO FETCHED IN THOSE DOGS"?

One time I felt sorry for a feller, Gus Langdon, brought in about 25 coon hides, but I couldn't buy them because the hair on them was pulling. They looked good but they had been hanging in the barn or somewhere and it had turned warm and ruined them. I told him I couldn't buy them and he insisted they were good but I couldn't do it . . . . I suppose he sold them somewhere. You had to watch that awful close. A lot of these older fellers would just skin them out and not salt them or anything. Just hang them in the barn and hides would go bad quick if you had a warm day or so in January. I wasn't in the fur business very long but I had a lot of fun and that is what I was in it for.

A few years ago Vic and I were out driving around and I said "I would like to go and look up ole Ed Bowers and see if he is still around". We went down there. It was south of Greenville, a little place called

Smithboro. I ought to remember that because it is the name of Vic's kinfolk. She was a Smith. We had got there and it had burned. I talked to a feller who lived in the house next to it. He said it had burned probably 10 years ago. I asked if they ever set business back up anywhere, he said Ed had died, and the boys went at it a while and then it burned out so they just let it go. So that was that!

A GOOD DOG THAT WENT BAD

By George Clark

When Max got his drivers license, I had an old Ford pickup truck 4 x 4 and he thought it would go anywhere and it did. He and Paul Kallenbach were good friends, Paul bought the ole plot dog from Brandenberg down by Hetrick II. I had an old blue tick bitch. She was pretty good but I didn't want her to run with every dog in the country. We took them out one night but that plot hound wouldn't leave the lantern light. We took her out several times but she would never leave the lantern light. I don't know if he got his money back or what, but anyway we had a litter of pups that we were selling. Max said lets give Paul a pup that could run with the mother. About that time I told Lloyd I would like to have an old dog that I could train pups with. Lloyd said, "well I have just the dog you need". I don't' know how old he was, but I kept him till he died. He didn't have papers but he was a good blue tick. He was true but he just got old. He would hunt good, but wasn't to fast. He would take pups out with him and if ya took another male out with him they would want to challenge him. He wasn't to backward. He could whip the pup out and put him in line. I would like to had him when he was young. That is what I was looking for. He was just a good old dog that you could handle good and when you got ready to go home he was ready to go home with ya. We gave Paul that pup and he was a good dog. He done good with that pup. Paul caught a lot of coons with that dog. He and Max were together a lot of times hunting. A lot of the boys were hunting with them, the Reich boys and Golly. He maybe even hunted with Breeze Mitchell once or twice. Max really enjoyed hunting. To bad kids now days when they are in the 8th grade or get into high school don't have a dog to hunt. You would know where they were at. It was a good feeling to have those boys out hunting instead of running the streets. Paul kept that dog for a long time. He kept him in a corn crib. One night Virgil (Paul's dad) went out to feed the dog and the dog took him. If Virgil hadn't got to the end of the chain the dog would have mauled him. The dog had never been that way before and don't understand why that happened, but Paul did end up having to put him down. We had several pups out of the female and sold a lot of them. One guy from up around Plymouth bought one, that he was very happy with. I sold a lot of pups and most were good dogs.

MY COON HUNT WITH OLIVER

By George Clark

It was probably 1962 or 63, I went to see my good friend Bob Kleinlein, while he was working at his shop, working on cars and tractors. It use to be the old Wolfmeyers Garage. He owned a plane and so did my brother Rolland, so many times we would just sit around visiting and gas a vehicle every now and then. We were sitting there talking in the garage and in walked his father Oliver Kleinlein, who had some age on him. He has passed away now. He was an ardent coon hunter. He set there awhile and said "do you boys want to go coon hunting tonight". Bob looked at me and said "well it looks like it's going to be a nice night". I am not a bad weather coon hunter. It was crisp but not a bad night, so Bob and I decided to go. Bob picked me up and we went down to Oliver's down on 107. He had a carp pond that everyone fished in, but come coon season, he was ready to go. I am not sure where we went but I think we ended up down by the old Kleinlein Place, which was northwest of where he lived. It was about 7:30 pm by the time we got to the woods. He had a good black and tan coon dog that everyone said was GOOD. I thought well, if he is as good as everyone says he is we ought to have a good night. We let the ole dog loose. It was a nice night to coon hunt. I had an old wheat light that I had for years an I still do. We sat there and talked a little bit and let the old dog track a little bit. Pretty soon the old dog hit a track. He had a good voice . . . . a very good voice.

You have heard people say that feller could skin a coon and never stop talking or never stop walking and ole Oliver could do just that. He could get the hide off a coon about as fast as anyone, outside Jr Utter or Lloyd Reische. I done quite a bit of hunting with Lloyd. He could get the hide off a coon pretty quick too! We hunted for quite awhile and it would have been up and down those ridges just south of McKee Creek. It was a good hunt. Now Oliver is quite a bit older than us, I wasn't to old. Oliver was in his 60's and about then I am telling ya it was hard to keep up with him. We hunted about 3 hours or maybe a little more. The dog never missed a lick, when he got to the tree he would let you know right now. I think we ended up with 3 coons that night. We got back to the car and he was ready to go. It was one of the nicest coon hunts I had been on in quite awhile. I usually took my kids, Max and Beth or went out with Lloyd Reische. He always wanted to coon hunt all night and I wasn't interested in that. The weather didn't make much difference to him either, he was always ready to go.

FUZZ & JEFF'S
COON HUNTING SCHEME

By Jeff Clark

I can remember one time when the school was having their annual FFA coon hunt. I'm not sure how you won, but I'm sure the biggest was in there somewhere. Well I'll start out by telling you that I am Fuzz Stolp's cousin, and I would help him clean hog houses every weekend, and we would hang out at his older brother Jims house in the evening also because Jim was never home. Well it happened to be the weekend of the annual FFA coon hunt and Fuzz and I thought we would win the hunt. We knew Jim had a big coon in his freezer that had not been skinned out. So we dug it out of the freezer, the problem being . . . the coon had to be killed the night of the hunt. Well Fuzz knew that it was going to be the biggest coon and he could win. So what does he do but wrap the coon in foil and sticks it in Jims oven to warm it up so he can take it in and get it weighed.. Well he did have the biggest coon until the last guy checked in and he beat Fuzz out! We lost Fuzz this year and this fond memories will stay with me till the end of time. But we sure had fun that night, and laughed about it for a long time.

GRAND NIGHT CHAMPION COON HUNT

By Jim Crook

Growing up in Pleasant View back in the 70 and 80's there wasn't a lot to do to make money, so coon hunting was a way to get extra cash for the local Graggs Store. One memorable night Charlie Hendricks, one of my brothers and I took Charlie's best coon dog out hunting. It was a Grand Night Champion. Charlie use to brag a lot on the dog. We hit the woods and wasn't there very long when the coon hound hit a track and away he went. He kept going and going until you could hardly hear him. Then no sound at all . . . Charlie said "he's on a ridge runner". I asked "a ridge runner, what is a ridge runner?". Charlie said "it's a jumbo coon that will run all night and the dog will never catch him". So Charlie laid down a blanket and left. The next day Charlie went back to the spot where we left the blanket and there was his hound dog laying on the blanket, completely worn out. What we found out later was that his ridge runner was a four legged coon with a big rack . . . . a deer that is. That dog hit that deer scent and never looked back till morning. We didn't get any coons that night, but I found out what a ridge runner was and a Grand Night Champion coon hunt was! Ha Ha Ha!!!

TEENAGE COONHUNTERS

By Darwin Dodds

The neighbor boy and I was 15 and 16 years old when we went hunting. He had a coon dog, 4 cell flashlight, kerosene lantern and a single shot one eyed rifle. I had nothing, but off we went. He had a female black and tan that he got from Sam Gust, who was a hunter back in his day.

Across the branch and up through the pasture we went. We were laughing and talking about school stuff, cause we didn't have any coon hunting stories to talk about. We got two coons that night. The next night we went to his uncles over on Sugar Creek. We were walking along the field when the dog hit a track. We stopped for a minute when the dog treed. Through the brush we run. He said "It sounds like heaven" and I said "It was hell!" I was getting hit upside the head by limbs, falling over roots and sticks. What a night we had. We got 10 coons, 5 up the first tree!.

I bought a 2 cell flashlight the next day. I was ready that night. We never got much that night. The weekend was gone, but we would slip out on school nights and hunt a night or two.

One evening we caught an albino coon. We thought it was a big old yellow cat when we first shined the tree, then we caught the ring on his tail, it was the only coon we got that night.

We hunted for the next three years until graduation. I quit coon hunting but he hunted the rest of his life. The other teenage boy was Jr Utter, probably the hardest hunter to hit the woods. All the stories you have heard are no doubt all true. He could skin a coon while walking stopping to pull the hide over the head and ears, staying out all night, getting lost, sleeping in fence rows, etc.

Later in years I got a dog or two and went hunting. Never had a good dog, but I had good lights. I would go with my uncle Bill Dodds some. He had some pretty good dogs over the years. We had some good and some bad hunts going with different hunters, but none like our teenage ones, toads going up your pant legs, being chased by cattle, not a care in the world.

Sixty years have passed, Jr has passed away, but the memories and the old oak tree on top of the hill still stands where we caught the albino coon.

FFA COON HUNT

By Larry Egbert

Dad, my 13 years old nephew Tim and I started on a the FFA coon hunt one night, I think it was 1978. When they going up the road they saw a coon and turned the dogs, Dolly and Sally loose, Then time was getting short because check in time at the school was midnight, so we started to Rushville through Kinderhook and saw a coon cross the road, we again turned the dogs on it and they treed a hundred yards from the road. We shot it out and it was a good size, it was a 18-20 lbs coon.

We all got there in time for weigh in and we tied for the biggest coon. With a flip of a coin we won. Tim was really proud to win the contest. To this day he can still remember the FFA coon hunt. He was so happy, Dad let him have the hide which he sold for $35-$40 dollars to Don Lerch the fur buyer at the station. This is a memory we will always cherish.

JANUARY THAW

By Larry Egbert

Dad and I were doing chores one late afternoon in January and there was a light snow on the ground and it was thawing. We both decided maybe the coons would be running tonight, so we decided not to go to far and headed southwest from home with dads dog "Dolly" and her pup "Sally". Dolly was the daughter of another blue tick male that Don Lerch owned.

Dolly wasn't hardly out of sight when she opened up west of the barn, then treed up a big white oak tree. We shined the tree and found two coon in the tree. One was an 18-20 lb sow coon which we figured came out of the barn, and the other one was a medium size male. That was a quick little hunt and we found out they run in mating season.

SCHUYLER COUNTY COON HUNTERS ASSOCATION 1979

Dad always like to take Dolly on the coon hunts and that year he placed second. I still have 4 trophy's he won with Dolly . . . a lot of good memories.

COON HUNTING WITH BEEEZE
By Don Fagan

Dick Powell, Breeze Mitchell and myself often went coon hunting together. This brisk winter night we traveled to Brown County to Breeze's place. Anyone who knows Breeze would know a good brisk wind would knock him over, as I don't think he weighed a hundred pounds soaking wet. He was always full of stories and kept hunting entertaining.

We were hunting down an old gravel road for easy walking. The dogs were turned loose and we would listen to hear them tree and compairing notes as to which dog was on a track, if one was running silent of if one was clear out of the race.

When we were sure the dogs had treed, we would follow their bark, locate the tree and shoot the coon. After much badgering about who was going to skin the coon and who had the sharp knife, Powell, of course, had to skin the coon, as I always seem to forget to bring my knife (or at least that's Powell's story).

We would then return to the end of the road and either lay down or sit on the ground talking, usually listening to Breeze tell stories and jokes, and listing for the dogs. Breeze had on a hunting coat that had a game bag on it that would open up without him knowing you were opening it. Every time we returned to the road to rest I would put some gravel in his game bag.

We treed three or four coons that night and were out several hours. On the last coon we went to the truck to go home and as Breeze was walking up the road he kept saying his coat was sure heavy for not having any of the coon hides in it. As he went to take his coat off gravel started falling out of the game pouch. Needless to say he wasen't very happy and in his good natured way gave me a royal cussing. But it was very good hunting

A RAINY NIGHT OF HUNTING

By Phil Fitzjarreld

My buddy Dan Norvell and I went to Kenny McDonalds farm one night just ahead of a real down pour. North of Kenny's house is a big hollow. We parked on the south side of the hollow, and away we went. The hunting was good that night, and then the rain came. We started back to the truck, and we ended up on the north side of the hollow with 9 coons and a ditch full of water. Soaking wet we walked back to the road and back to the truck.

On the way home the rain stopped and Dan said "lets go through Huntsville and hit Rudy's feed lot". Rudy's feed lot was 7 acres or more. After hunting the feed lot we got 8 more coons. It was muddy, but we caught coons. Our lead dog was a blue tick named Breezy. This little dog was a well know coon dog amongst coon hunters

SOMETHINGS YOU DON'T FORGET

By Steve Ford

A normal late November evening calm and cold. As I put the dogs in the truck I knew it was going to be one of those nights. As the dogs were buckled in I shut the tailgate and shut my finger in the tailgate, after a little ice and a bandied, off we went.

Twenty minutes down the road—almost there a deer almost hit us. What else was going to happen. Dad looked at me and said "It's going to be a good night", "sure it is" I replied.

No sooner than we got there and turned the dogs out they put one up the tree—so I thought. After a short walk through the blackberry briers we found Ole Red and BT (black & tan) searching the big white oak we found eyes. After finding an open spot to shoot-down came the coon. The dogs of course were all over it like ugly on a ape. A nice big sow.

As dad and I started to walk away dad stopped, turned around and looked back at the white oak tree, the dang tree had eyes all over it. So about 45 minutes to an hour later and 5 more ringtails, dad said he had enough and it was time to go home. However it must have been all of the excitement or cold I had to take a leak. I turned off my light, turned around, took 4 or 5 steps and let it go. A short time later I got the shock of my life, HOT WIRE!! Dad was right when he said there are some things you don't forget.

This is only one of many coon hunting memories of Lyle and Steve Ford.

JOHN SPATES

By Marian Fretueg

My father, John Spates, began coon hunting at a very young age. He would hunt with his father, R.A. Spates, as well as friends. One particular story I remember my grandmother Minnie Spates sharing with me was one instance when Daddy went coon hunting with his father and Carl Brooks as a grade schooler. They got lost or just simply lost track of time and did not arrive home until 4:30 in the morning. Grandma was extremely mad that they had kept John out so late. Daddy thought she would let him stay home from school that day, not my Grandma! She made him get up and go to school that day.

In addition to coon hunting, my father also bought and sold coon hides. Daddy ran Spates Produce and Creamery in the 1950's and early 1960's. Local hunters would bring their coons and Daddy would pay them for their hides. He had a place set up in the back room of the shop where he skinned the coons and dressed the carcasses. In my mind, I can still see him skinning those coons, and wonder exactly how many he actually did skin over the years. He would put the carcasses in the cooler and when we traveled to Peoria to sell cream, Daddy would stop at bars in Peoria to sell the coon carcasses. Many times, my sister Lydia and I would sit in the truck waiting for Daddy to come out of the bar while he went in to sell carcasses.

There were several people Daddy hunted with throughout the years. Those I remember most were Lee Herche and Paul Busby. In addition to hunting, with friends, Daddy also partnered up with his coon dogs. He had several different coon dogs throughout his lifetime, but only one dog at a time. The first one I remember was named Roscoe. The next was named Sam after Sam Gust, who he had gotten the dog from. He had named one Penny and the last one he had was named Brit.

Daddy would prepare to go coon hunting as soon as supper was over. He would gather all his hunting gear together. The one thing I remember most was the smell of his carbide light. He would attach the light to his hat. His dog, whichever one it was at the time, was always ready to go hunting and would practically pull Daddy to the car to get into the trunk to go hunting. Daddy would always use the car and one time he even had a special vent put in to make sure his dog had enough air. There were nights he wouldn't get home until after midnight. If his dog didn't come back to him before Daddy was ready to come home he would leave a rug for the dog to lie on. The next morning Daddy would go back to pick up his dog.

I never actually went coon hunting with him in the woods but there were a couple of times coons would come up to the back of the house and Brit would tree them. Daddy and I would go out and I would hold the light and he would shoot the coon.

One time when he was hunting with his dog, Brit, she didn't come in when Daddy was ready to go home. He left the rug and went back to pick her up the next day. Brit was not there but Daddy kept returning to check on her. He visited all the homes in the surrounding area where he had been hunting and even put a lost and found ad in the paper. Finally, after much time had passed, he just gave up and assumed something must have happened to her. Much to Daddy's surprise, a year later Brit was found. She had been taken in by a farmer. Daddy got his coon dog back. She died in 1991 and Daddy never went coon hunting again. Coon hunting was a big part of Daddy's life. He enjoyed hunting very much.

JJ'S LAST HUNT
By Danny Hanning

I will tell of a night when we just plain had a good time. At this time gas was under a dollar a gallon and we liked to take two trucks, and leave one on each end of our intended hunt. I was hunting with Jack Kelly and our old buddy Larry (JJ) Prather decided he wanted to go with us on this night. Now JJ wasn't a coon hunter so we saw this as an opportunity for some fun. Not having his own light, JJ would follow along behind us getting slapped with every limb and brier bush there was. Every now and then he would ask for a light and we were more than happy to shine two of them back in his face. He accused us of doing this on purpose, but I'm sure we were just trying to help. I think we caught 3 or 4 coons on our hunt when we came to the other truck. The night was young so we stopped at Leroy Fitzjarrald's house to visit house to visit awhile. We started playing cards and having a nip or two. It was soon one thirty in the morning and time to go home. On standing, it was clear I had too much whiskey in my coffee. As we started for home I told the boys I need to hunt awhile before we went home to sober up a bit. This comment met with much resistance, but we were in my truck so I just let them howl.

I made up my mind where I wanted to dump out and on our way there was a coon crossing the road in front of us. This was a good sign that they were still moving and I knew I was dumping out again one way or the other. We made our way to Wildcat Slough. We hunted there quite a bit. Several times we would run track up the Slough and then loose it. I parked the truck and got out but my companions stayed in the truck. It was cold and they were whiney and refused to come. I reached behind the seat and got a shotgun, because I was going by myself and couldn't see quite straight. As soon as the dogs hit the ground they opened up on a track. With this, Jack decided to come along but JJ still sat in the truck. I took the keys with me as I wanted the truck to be there when we returned.

As in the past the track went right to the end of the Slough and the dogs faltered. Now I remember I told you it was cold and the Slough was frozen hard. We coaxed the dogs out on the ice and they picked the track back up and the race was back on. We continued up the Slough for at least half a mile maybe more when the dogs finally treed. Now is when I was really lucky Jack had come along because even on a good night he could find coons I could not.

It was a big tree up on the bluff. Soon enough Jack said "I got one, and another, and another, and another" they were all bunched up together. I was glad I didn't take my 22, as the first shot with the shotgun didn't bring out a single coon. This brought out a laugh from Jack at my expense!! I had to bear down and manage to get all four out with the next four shots. We had an old sow and most of her litter, I don't know why they were still with her, as they were as big as she was.

We started skinning coons and laughing about the track, wondering how many times this old sow had tricked us at the slough in the past. I guess I forgot about JJ. We got back to the truck about 4:00 am tired and sobered up, ready to go home. The truck windows were all frosted over, when I opened the door, the cussin began. JJ was sitting there with his hood pulled up over his face freezing his butt off. I reminded him we were both warm, if he had come with us he would be as well. This statement didn't improve his disposition at all!!. Jack and I both took much pleasure in this but JJ just couldn't find the humor in it. We finally collected Jack's truck and got home. I don't know why but we could never get JJ to go hunting with us again.

THE BIG ONE

By Danny Hanning

I would like to tell about a night when I was most proud of my dogs. Now at this time I was hunting two dogs, Veda and a small red tick marked cross bred dog. My sister had raised her own on a bottle so you can imagine our connection with her. Now Veda was a small, fine boned dog, completely silent. When you heard her bark, it was time to shoot. The other dog was Roscoe, half hound and half catahula stock dog, a bruit who loved his muscle his way along. Both dogs were hot nosed, and very tight hunters. I never went over a quarter of a mile to get to the tree.

This night we hunted at home. As we passed a familiar den tree in the pasture and they struck a track. This was nothing new and I was sure we had ran this track before. We proceeded through the timber and made it through to Cedar Creek. It was a tough track, up on logs, under, up and down the creek bank, watching the dogs work I finally found the coon tracks in the sand. It was huge. I remember saying to my dogs "We won't get this one, you two aren't smart enough". Well the track didn't go much further and Veda hit a tree that goes up a little ways then leans out sharply over the creek. I looked it over good and could not find a coon, but the dogs were sure and would not give up. I finally picked out a knot where the tree reached out over the creek that just did not look right. I looked through the scope of my rifle but still didn't see a coon. I decided to take a shot and see what happened. One shot, and I heard that all familiar PLUNK!! That told me we had him, but he did not move. The second shot got his attention and he came out, not a bit happy. Now at this point Veda, by herself would have been in trouble, but with Roscoe this was his strength. The fight didn't last long and we had one of the biggest coons I ever caught.

The night was young and we were a long way from the house so we kept hunting. I'm sure we caught several more coons that night, but I don't remember because it didn't matter, because we had caught the big ole boy who had challenged us before and went home proud and happy.

OLE DUTCH AND AL

By Al Hamilton

Harold Boyd had a 19 year old blue tick hound that was a wonderful coon dog and really enjoyed tracking and treeing those ole raccoons, and he was going strong at the age of 19 and has had a trailing and treeing sound I dearly loved. Harold wanted me to hunt him as he was retiring from hunting. I hunted with Harland Terry on his land. This night we treed a large female coon and two young ones in a den tree. I had to climb up and look down in the hollow tree and shot them. Then we couldn't retrieve them, so Harland said since it was on his land, to mark the tree where they were and he would come back the next day with the tractor and take his tractor and chain saw and get them out, so I marked the tree. I told him to be sure not to saw into them. So the next night when I got there he had them laying down on the ground, belly down. He had sawed right through the large ones belly which ruined its hide. So his wife was a very good seamstress, so I knocked on the door and held up the hide and said to her "could you sew this hide on your sewing machine", and she said "no way". Well we took them to Don Lerch to sell them and was careful to keep them face down and he said "it looks like you got a big one this time" but being a good fur buyer the first thing he did was turn them over and the price went down right away!

ALWAYS RELEASE

By Wendy Logsdon Hillyer

It was a cool winter night in November 1983, when I was on my very first coon hunting adventure. I say adventure, because coon hunting is like no other hunting sport. My dad Bob Logsdon is an avid hunter, so I was raised to hunt, but again I was not sure what coon hunting had in store for me. Here is my story . . .

That cool winter night my dad, Wendell Stritzel, his daughter Kellee and I were going on this coon hunting adventure. Getting prepared for coon hunting seemed to be like any other hunting sport, except the barking dogs, the light and it was dark! Heading to the woods I remember asking questions of both my father and Wendell, "how do I do this?" "how do I do that"? Kellee, who has hunted many night with her dad, just laughed at me for asking so many questions, she was an avid coon hunter herself. We arrived at the site and began to unload the dogs and get our guns ready. I was given one of the dogs on a leash, simple job I thought. Boy was I wrong! Heading deep in the woods, following my dad, Wendell and Kellee I thought to myself, this don't seen to hard at all. Well as any coon hunter may know, or at least a new one it is much harder than you think. As we got deep in the holler I met my first unseen tree limb and ended up falling on the ground with a dog staring me in the face.

Laughs! Who would have known even the dog was thinking. "This 14 year old girl has no clue how to coon hunt"! I picked myself back up thinking I really need to use this flashlight much better next time. The dogs that were not on leashes began to hunt, as Wendell and my dad started their conversation, "I think this may be the one". The dogs began to bark and control the scent of getting the coon. The word "RELEASE" was called out, though I did not hear it or understand the meaning of the word. I bet you are wondering what happened, well let me tell you all what happened.

As all the dogs were hunting this coon they all had their keen sites, the dog I had still on the leash and did not understand the meaning of the word "RELEASE" began to do what he knew to do and that was RUN and HUNT. Well, let me tell you when a good coon dogs knows what to do he goes full force hunting that coon for his owner, I just happened to be drug behind him for many yards as my hand was wrapped inside the handle of the leash. This was not a fun place to be at that given moment with many things in my path. Finally my dad and Wendell was able to get to the dog, at that moment I felt like I was being saved from all the debris that was in my path.

As you can imagine what happened next with three very skilled coon hunters looking at this first timer. Well we got the coon and I got my first adventure under my belt in coon hunting. I will forever remember that "RELEASE" means just that, release the dog and let him hunt. We live and learn from our mistakes in our adventures in life and I learned so much from that night, and after all these years I still remember it like it was yesterday and I became a good hunter because I learned to pick myself up and listen to the ones that knew so much.

A MEMORABLE COON HUNT

By Byron Hull

It began on one of those perfect fall nights for coon hunting, big yellow moon with just enough clouds passing over it to dim its brightness. My hunting buddy, Olin, and I worked second shift at Beardstown's Oscar Meyer plant and were very anxious to get home, grab our coon hounds, and hit the woods.

Olin had a young dog that he wanted to run along side my old faithful Walker hound "Nick". If I do say so myself, and I always did, Nick was one of the best coonhounds in the country. Heck, maybe in the whole state! He had a hot nose, a beautiful trailing bark and a consistent "chop" when he treed. Nick had many hides and trophies to his credit. He had one blue eye and one brown eye and they just looked like they held the hunting wisdom of the ages. I swear sometimes those eyes would twinkle when he picked up a coon's scent and began tracking. I could trust old Nick to do his best every time.

That night, we had walked about a half mile before Nick struck a coon. He took off like a rocket and Olin's pup followed along for the joy of the run, even if he didn't know quite what it was all about yet. Nick chased Mr. Coon along the creek bottom and finally up the hill to an old tree that had the top broken out. Olin caught up with the dogs and looked up at the fat old coon perched up high in the broken tree trunk.

Figuring the coon would fall down after being shot, I raised my rifle and fired. Sure enough the coon disappeared from view. Nick was going crazy and Olin was about as bad.

"Where'd he go, Barney? Where did that blasted coon go?" Olin was a self proclaimed "Missouri Hillbilly", tall and lanky, and never without his old pipe stuck in his teeth. Right now he was hopping up and down like a banny rooster looking for that ole coon.

We decided the coon must have fallen into some sort of crevice in the old tree instead of falling to the ground, so we went closer to investigate. We walked around the tree and found a hole just about head level. Olin stuck his hand inside and couldn't feel anything. It was getting cloudier so we couldn't really see much of anything. Pulling his hand away, Olin felt a stream of blood so we knew the rifle had hit its target. We shot the coon . . . so where was it?. Being the dedicated coon hunter he was, Olin decided to stick his whole head into the hole and try to see what was going on. I think he removed his pipe from his mouth, but to this day I am not sure.

What I am sure about was poor old Olin got his head stuck . . . totally lodged in the hole in the side of the tree. At first I was worried that the coon might be in there and would go after Olin, but when that didn't seem to be the case, I just lost it! I laughed and stomped and finally rolling on the ground. I had never treed anything so big before. Of course, Olin was not laughing! He was yelling, "Get me out of here, you fool! Help me!" and both dogs were barking and jumping all over him. I had to grab him by the legs and pick him up so he could turn his head and pull himself out of the hole. He wasn't amused, but he was a mess. He had blood from the coon on his hands and his face and his hat was gone and his hair was standing on end. About then we heard something from the backside of the tree and old Mr. Coon reappeared and took off like lighting. The dogs were off again chasing him through more dense timber. This time the dogs caught up with the coon and made short work of him. The little pup seemed to come into his own and ran like a pro.

We treed and shot two more coons that long ago fall night and I think Olin's pup learned some valuable lessons in hunting. He went on to become an excellent coon hound with many hides and trophies of his own. But I think the greatest lesson was learned by Olin himself that night, don't stick your fool head in a hole in a tree! "A hole in one" is for golfers . . . not coon hunters! We all got back home safe and sound with our bounty . . . and with a great story of "A Memorable coon hunt".

AL AND THE HOLLOW TREE

By Maynard Hulvey

I started coon hunting in the early sixties, about that time, they were starting to use carbide lights instead of kerosene lanterns. We carried our carbide in a Prince Albert tobacco can and a little bottle of water to keep our lights going. Later we went to wheat lights.

I hunted with Wayne Morrell, my father-in-law, Bill Crum, Dick Powell, and Bob Forsythe. We would come in from hunting at twelve or one o'clock in the morning and sometimes the wives would have pie and coffee.

In the seventies, I hunted with Al Hamilton. He had a three legged blue tick dog and I had two blue ticks. We treed a coon one night in a hollow tree. It had a big hole in the bottom. Al sticks his head in, sees the coon, takes my pistol, jams his head and shoulders in the hole, and shoots the coon. We were standing there and didn't hardly hear the shot. Then Al came out of the hole, rolled around on the ground and we though he had shot himself. But it was his ears, he couldn't hear the rest of the night.

There was a fur buyer by the name of Lyle Stratton, he came to Al's house and picked up coons every morning. The highest I ever got for a coon was $28.00 dollars.

THE RIVER HUNT

By Kenny Jamison

It was Friday after Thanksgiving 1987. Two friends, Tommy Lanter, Larry Thomas and I decided to go coon hunting. Tom had a blue tick named Jake. Jake was 4 years old and very good at putting you on a tree and he never lied. I wanted to go to Thurman holler and my buddies wanted to go to the river bottoms, We headed across the river and through Allen ditch. About half way through the ditch I see eyes. I put the boat on the bank and turned the dogs loose. By the time I tied the boat up and put a light on it so we would know where the boat was, the dogs had treed. Larry hollered and said "I see two in this tree, and Tom sees one, and Jake is on the big one". I stayed with Jake and knocked the coon out and Jake had about all he could handle. I handed Tom the gun, he shot, and out came the coon. Jake grabbed that coon up and shook him, then looked up the tree waiting for another one. Tom handed me the gun, "I cannot see him, can you? Yes I can" I said. I shot but left some fight in this one, about four shakes and Jake broke his neck. We headed to Larry at another tree Jake let us know there was a coon in the tree. I got behind Larry and shined the light. "I see two eyes, I shot and out came the coon, then I looked up and there was one more coon in that tree. This coon ran up the tree and jumped out, and Jake was waiting for him. The coon bit Jake on the leg, Jake didn't like that one bit! When Jake grabbed him the next time by the back of the neck and that was the end of that coon. Tom asked where the boat was, I pointed over to my right and said "look for the light". You always want to leave a light on the boat at night, it would be to easy to loose your boat. Jake started treeing again, Larry said "I see two sets of eyes in different parts of the tree. Then we had trouble seeing them, and we finally seen them through the scope. We shot and out came a big ole sow coon on her back legs and bit Jake, and then Jake made short work of her. We then headed back to the boat. When we got to the boat I lite the lantern and hung it on a limb. Tom started skinning coons and tells Larry to put Jake an a lead, I was getting us a drink out of the cooler and before I got Jake on a lead I saw eyes on the bank. Larry grabbed the gun and more shells. He said

"I think we brought more drinks than shells" Jake trees the coons about 200 ft apart, we shot the coons and Jake finished them off, and back to the boat we headed. When we got back to the boat Tom was getting all of us a drink, he handed Larry the knife and a pair of pliers and he ask what these were for, Tom told him he could skin for awhile "I came for a drink and a boat ride" Larry said "I'll skin them as soon as I drink this. We got back in the boat and went up the river and back to the Schuyler side across from Riverside Gun Club. Tom immediately sees a coon, Jake was in the back of the boat, ran to the front and out the boat he went! We got to the bank and Larry and Tom left me to tie up the boat and hang the light. I started loading clips with shells and I hear laughing. When I got to them Tom is cussing Larry to help him up, Tom is flat on his back in black river bottom gumbo. I had to laugh. We found a tree limb to help him out. We scraped mud off of Tom and he cleaned out his boots, I said "I had to laugh, but you are a mess. When we got to where Jake was treeing there were 3 coons about 20 and 50 feet up, and they were big coons. Tom shot three times and he fell and Jake done his thing thinking it was dead, well he found out it wasn't, the coon bit him right on his nose and lip. When the coon let loose Jake grabbed him by his neck and finished him. Tom looked Jake over and thought he was ok. Larry ask Tom if he would sell Jake, Larry said "you wouldn't hunt him" Tom replied "no, but I would teach him to drink and crunch cans!" Tom wanted to change cloths so we went back to the landing. Jake ran down the river and treed 2 coons under the coal chute. As I am getting the gun out of the case Larry got close to the coal chute and one of the coons jumped down and runs between Larry's legs and so does Jake knocking Larry in the river. I killed the other coon while Jake trees the other one up a light pole. I shot it off the light pole laughing the hole time about Larry being knocked in the river. We started up the river at the mouth of Sugar Creek, there were eyes on the bank. Jake hit the ground barking, we got 3 coons out of the first tree, and Jake was about 50 yards away and treeing again. He didn't wait to be shot he jumped out of the tree and Jake took care of him. He had a good laugh about that. Farther back from the river Larry shot 2 more coons, we gathered up our coons and trying to think how many coon we had seen. Jake went down the river and treed on a big maple tree. I dug out 2 clips and 14 bullets is all I could scrounge up. Tom and Larry were already at the tree, I ask them if they had seen any coons, Tom said he had seen two and Larry had seen a big one. Tom said to knock them out dead since you only have 14 bullets left, and to make each one count. Jake wasn't to pleased with that decision. We gathered up and went back to the boat, had a drink and I was ready to call it a night, but Tom said let's go around Sugar Creek Island, so up the river we went on the Schuyler side. Tom shines his light on the bank and there are coon, one big coon stands up on his back legs. Jake sees them and as soon as we hit the bank he is out the boat and hit the ground running. We tied up and put up the light, and went through the timber and through a corn field along the edge, Jake had already treed. Larry fell down in a pile of cornstalks, and I asked him if my gun was ok, he said "I need help up, if the gun is broken you will be climbing trees! I get back to the tree, aim, and shoot, out comes the coon. The gun had fired ok, I told Larry he was lucky, we shot 2 more out and headed back to the boat.

We went around the upper end of the island, we were floating inside the island with no lights on. Tom was complaining about skinning coons tonight. I turned on my light halfway down the island, and there were eyes, we started the engine and went to the bank, and Jake treed within 50 yards. Larry and Tom went to the tree and got one coon. When we got back to the boat, Tom trips over the pile of coons and says "I think we have a load." We were floating again and saw a coon dragging in a fish, I hollered "coon!" and Jake was on the bow of the boat, we were about 40 yards from the coon. Larry is getting the gun out and we move along side of the coon and Jake jumps on top of it. Both Jake and the coon was in deep water. Tom yelled "get that dog in the boat." I took the engine out of gear, grabbed Jake by the collar and then I had the coon trying to climb up Jake and my arm. Larry hit's the coon with the end of the gun, knocking him off of Jake. Tom was holding Jake, and the coon was headed back to the bank, and us behind him. Jake is on the bow, held by Tom, the coon hit's the bank with us right behind him, Tom let Jake go and he killed the coon. We got the boat loaded and had a good laugh about this one. We headed back to Frederick Landing, at the coal trussel there were two sets of eyes glowing at us, Tom says "let it go", so up the hill we went to go to Beardstown, when we get to my place we started eating and having a cold drink. What a night that was, I will never forget it. I talk to Tom every once in awhile, he lives in southern IL and works in Kentucky, Tom still coon hunts and has never had another dog like Jake. Larry is hunting ducks up in heaven, cancer got the best of him in 1999. This is one of my most memorable coon hunts.

JUST GLAD TO BE OUT OF THE RAIN

By Gary Kennedy

My coon hunting started about 40 years ago. I had permission to hunt on a neighbor's land. Nowdays, you don't know your neighbor's they all live out of state and don't like neighbor's.

I had a not-so-understanding wife in early years, couldn't understand the thrill of the dogs runnin'. Later, after a few years, she was glad to see me go. I'm probably the only hunter that had that problem!

I hunted with Jack Kelly early on, a great hunting partner. We had great hunts with the dogs making no mistakes, then we had other hunts. We hunted every kind of dog we even had a beagle that treed pretty good. In all out hunts, we won one hunt with the biggest coon.

I remember one rainy night, Jack and I were headed out of the bottom around Wild Cat Slough. In the headlights, we saw a man walking towards us. We stopped and it was our game warden. I had my pistol under my coat, loaded naturally. John slid in the truck, hitting my gun with his arm. He never said a word. I think the ride out of the rain was more important at the time. I haven't been coon hunting for many, many years, but I now have a grandson who has his own dogs and they hunt.

LIFETIME MEMORIES WITH DAD
By Jeff Kennedy

As a young boy growing in a small farm town, I was always with my dad. It didn't matter if we were doing chores, checking crops, riding horses, or just driving to a neighbor's house to say hi, we were a pair. Coon hunting was no different. He couldn't get out of the house without me. On school nights, my mon would argue that I should stay home. She often won. However there were many school nights we were hunting, but we promised as early return. On one occasion, I ended up in the hospital with pneumonia, having begged my mom to let me go for a while and having a slight fever.

I think my best memories of coon hunting as a young boy were the nights I would lay down to rest. Nestea plunge style, into the snow, and staring up at th sky. Of course if there wasn't any snow on the ground, I would be more careful, but the end results always the same. Our dog would be "on track" and this was our chance to stop and listen. While laying down, I would gaze at the stars or the moon, no doubt asking 50 questions about what I was seeing or hearing. Just then it would happen. "He's treed, let's go son!"

I tried hard to keep up, usually moving a pretty good clip. I'm sure my dad would get frustrated waiting on me or helping be over barbed wire fence, but he never let it be known. Up hills, down hills, crossing the frozen streams, and finally we get to the tree. "There he is, see his eyes? The dogs were in a frenzy as we were all excited. Then I would hear "pop", the 22 rifle had been fired. Just like in slow motion, the coon fell from the tree. The dogs would attack and finish the job. After we would catch the dogs and congratulate them on a completed mission, my dad would smile and pick up the coon and say "good job boys, dead coon, let's go home" These are memories that I will carry with me the rest of my life.

SAM CAME HOME

By Dave Kilpatrick

In the mid 70's my father-in-law William "Bill" Bartlett thought it would be great to own a coon hound. The cost of hides was way up, plus there was all the excitement of following a dumb dog through all the multi-floral roses in hot pursuit while packing knives, balin wire, and extra carbide for your lantern in your back pack.

As I recall he found this Black and Tan up around Plymouth. Next thing needed was a kennel (which is still there at the farm house). I pitched in pouring the concrete and setting the posts and wire. With that accomplished we went to Plymouth to get "Sam". Was we ever excited to own such a great dog. As it turns out, he was a pretty damn good hound with one hellva nose. However, he only had one slight flaw. You had to hope the first thing he smelled after you started hunting was a coon. If a fresh deer scent hit his nose first you just as well go home.

To my best recollection we first discovered this slight problem about the 4th or 5th time out. As usual we headed east of the barn into the bottoms of Stoney Branch Creek. We had been having good hunts towards Gale Hoods place. We had crossed the creek and Sam hit a hot trail, so off he went with us in hot pursuit. After a few minutes we realized the barking seemed to be getting farther and farther away until we couldn't head him at all. We walked and called then walked and called some more. Finally a couple of hours later we came out at Gale's house and went back home on the road. This was the best part of the hunt so far as there weren't any briars on the road. Three days went by and Bill was just positive his new dog was lost, never to be heard from again, and then Sam just showed up. From his very dirty condition and obvious weight loss we assumed that he finally gave up on the deer and actually tracked a coon into a ground den and got stuck in the hole. He gave him a few days rest and extra rations to get his strength and back to par and off we went again the next weekend.

All in all, good times were had for the next several years out on the coon hunts.

MY BLUETICKS
By Gus Lashbrook

I have been hunting since I was 7 years old. My dad took me hunting with him and his two Black and Tan hounds. I loved it and have been hunting ever since.

I started out with several different breeds of dogs. I finally settled with Blue Tick hounds after hunting with another hunter who raised Blue Ticks. I liked the way they worked. They always hunted close to only took off when they had a good track. My first Blue Tick was a dog named Queen. Later I got a pup from Queen and named her Duchess.

Duchess turned out to be a real good strike dog, but a little weak on treeing.

One night we got permission to go hunting on a farm near my house. As soon as we kicked the dogs out, in no time they hit a track. My buddy's dog was a good tree dog. Once he got to the tree he wanted the coon so badly he started chewing on the tree and got a chunk of bark stuck in the roof of his mouth. We had to get the stick out of his mouth before shooting the coon out of the tree.

Next they treed in a large Oak tree which it was leaning at a 45 degree angle. Once again he got so excited he ran right up into the tree to the first fork. He was treeing on a limb where the coon was sitting, probably 25 feet off the ground. We had to call him down in order to shoot the coon, before he fell out himself. It was always an exciting time listing to the dogs, knowing you would soon have a coon up the tree.

THE MISSING COON HOUNDS

By Alan Lerch

When I was around 10 years old, I lived with my parents, Carl and Donna in Cuba, Illinois. My grandparents Byron "Pink" and Leila Irwin lived in Oakland twp. In Schuyler County. We moved from Rushville to Cuba in 1961 and visited my grandparents often. Both of my grandpa's loved to go coon hunting. There is a road that goes from Vermont to where my grandpa farmed, this is the route we usually took because it was the shortest. It is a narrow gravel road with a few blind corners. As we were traveling down the road we went around one of these blind corners and noticed two dogs lying next to the road by a light pole, then we noticed that the very top was a very large coon looking down at the dogs. I asked dad if he thought they might be grandpa's dogs, and he said he wasn't sure. We continued on to the farm, which was probably another mile or two. Shortly after we arrived, grandpa started telling us that he was really worried about his coon hounds. He said they had been missing for at least two days. He told us he had walked to the woods calling them by name with no results. It was not like them to stay gone very long and he was afraid something bad had happened to them. I could see that he was really upset. I said "grandpa, I think I know where your dogs are". When I told him I think they have a coon treed up a light pole, he first looked relieved and then he began +to laugh. He could hardly believe it. At that point we headed out to find two dog chains and off we went in his pickup truck. When we got to the dogs, we found they had barked until they were horse and could no longer utter a sound. Grandpa put the chains on them and had to pull them to the truck, they sure didn't want to leave that coon on the pole. Grandpa figured the coon had suffered enough being up the pole for two days or more without food or water. We returned home and he rewarded two very weary hounds with all the food and water they could hold. This is only one of the fond memories I have of spending time with my grandparents on their farm.

MY FIRST COON HUNT

By Bert Lerch

Did you ever have to do anything you didn't like to do? Well, I never really liked to go coon hunting, but my dad, Mike, loved to go every chance he could. He not only like to hunt for the sport but he sold hides and my mom cooked the meat. My mom really knew how to cook, it was really good. Dad always liked for us boys to go with him and I was getting to the age where it was my turn. One of the reasons I didn't like to go was it was cold that time of year and we would stay out for hours until we got them ole coons. We had two old faithful coon dogs, Old Buck and Trixie, who usually never let us down. In order to be a good coon hunter you had to have good dogs. After all, they were the ones that treed them and eventually got them.

One cold winter night about 6:00 pm my dad decided it was my turn to go coon hunting with him. We got our coats and caps on and picked up our flashlights, guns, Old Buck and Trixie and went off into the night. We lived on a farm and the woods was not to far from the house so we started out. We no more than got into the woods and Old Buck hit a coon track. About that time Trixie came to help. They spotted that coon and they chased him for a mile or so and finally treed him. Well, me just being a young boy felt sorry for the coon cause I knew what was going to happen to him when they got a hold of him. Anyway, dad and I had a ways to walk before we got to the tree. Ol Buck and Trixie stayed right there until we got there. The poor coon was so frightened all you could see was two black eyes staring into the night. That wasn't the end of the story, there were two more coons in the tree. What a surprise!! So we really hit the jackpot. Dad had a 16 gauge double barrel shotgun so I don't need to tell you what happened next. He shot those coons right out of the tree. I'll tell you Old Buck and Trixie was proud of themselves. The only problem was now we had to carry them the rest of the night and they got pretty heavy before the night was over. By this time I was getting tired and ready to go home. I thought we had done real good for this night. After all it was my first time to go hunting. I think that was the problem, we had done too good and dad decided to send Old Buck and Trixie to find another coon trail. By this time I think the dogs were getting tired to. We waited and we waited and we waited and they did not return so we decided to go find them. We finally found them laying at the base of the tree. We thought oh boy they have treed another coon, well they had, but they were so tired they were resting and the coon was still up in the. Dad shot him out, and seeing that the dogs were worn out, dad decided it was time to go home. We had a good night.

COON HUNTING
By Bert Lerch

Well the first hunting trip wasn't to bad. I had heard stories from the guys that went and it sounded like they sure had a good time. I knew some of the things they were telling were just like fish stories, the more you tell the bigger they got. The only difference is, it is harder to get them as they sure get heavy carrying them. Some of them we got would weigh 25-30 lbs. and sometimes we would get 3 or 4. Dad approached me again and said "son, lets go hunting tonight". I really wasn't in the mood but I remember the other time we went wasn't really that bad so I said "ok dad". Of course he had to pick another one of those cold nights to go but by this time I learned if I went with the attitude that this was going to be good night, that we would get several coons. I don't think so much about the cold weather. After all the more coons we got the more money we would make and the more of that good meat we would have to eat. We ate supper and it was dark when we got through so we dressed warmly, got the light, the gun and picked up Old Buck and Trixie and off we went through the woods. I was thinking in my mind, I hope this is night dad will let me try to shoot a coon. Little did I know he had already planned to let me do just that. It wasn't long before Old Buck and Trixie hit a coon trail and off they went. We stood there for about 15 minutes listing and finally heard them, they had treed a coon. Off we went to find them, it didn't take long. When we got there dad shined the light up in the tree and we didn't see a coon anywhere. I ask dad where the coon was and he said "see that hole up there in the tree, that ole coon is probably nestled down in that hole and won't come out till we are gone." He was right, he didn't. I couldn't see him to shoot him so I didn't get my first coon that night. That made me more eager to go the next time, now all I could think about was getting my first coon. The next night was to be the fateful night. I didn't wait for dad to ask me to go hunting, I asked him and he agreed to go. We went through our regular ritual again, we dressed warmly, picked up the light, and guns and got Old Buck an Trixie and off to the woods we went again. By this time Buck and Trixie were really getting excited so we knew they had hit another coon track. I was getting pretty excited because I knew this was probably going to be the big night for me. It wasn't long before they treed. I'll say one thing about them dogs, you would have to look a long time before you found better coon dogs. Dad cautioned me not to get so excited or I wouldn't be able to aim the gun and hit the coon. I told him he didn't realize how ready I was to get me a coon. We found the dogs and sure enough there was a coon in the tree. Dad shined the light up in the tree so I could see him and I cocked my gun, ready to shoot and he looked straight at me, two of the biggest black eyes I had ever seen, frightened black eyes, and I just froze! I could not pull the trigger. I could not shoot that coon that night. We went many times after that and I shot my share of coons. Some of my best memories I have of my dad and me were spent in the timber going coon hunting and I will treasure them forever. I never hunted again after I grew up, it just wasn't the same

Don Lerch, Dick Bowers and Rambler in 1977

Don Lerch as a young boy with Brownie & Blue

A good night of hunting with my Dad, Brownie & Blue in the 50's

MEMORIES WITH DAD & BUCK

By Carl Lerch

Memories of my dad, Mike Lerch always bring back thoughts of when we went coon hunting. My dad sometimes hunted for pleasure and sometimes out of necessity. I am number five of ten children. Our amount of Christmas depended on how many coon hides dad could sell before Christmas arrived. The best hunting dog dad ever owned was called "Buck". He was a large and strong and great at tracking and treeing coons and faithful to his master. My dad had a coat that was double material in the back and open on both sides for carrying as many as three coons. When dad hung this coat on our back porch, Buck allowed no one but him to touch it.

On one very dark night we decided it would be a good night to hunt. We got our gear together and set out with Buck leading the way. My dad had a carbide miners lamp on his cap, my brother Bert and I were following him with a very dim kerosene lantern. We entered an area of woods that was quite brushy making it very hard to see. Buck hit a coon track and dad began walking faster with my brother and I trying hard to keep up. Suddenly the earth seemed to drop from beneath my feet and I was falling, not realizing it was there I had stepped off a bank and fell into a dry creek. I was shaken, but not hurt, so we continued the hunt. Needless to say I do not remember rather or not we got the coon. However I remember how it felt to fall off a small cliff. There was one hunt that I wished I had been on and wasn't because I missed all the fun. We lived eight miles north of Rushville and my dad was hunting with a close friend and neighbor, Bryon "Pink" Irwin, who later became my father-in-law. They were hunting on a farm owned by Earl Wells, not far from where we lived. Mr. Wells raised a lot of black angus cattle, as usual you hunted the darkest nights and black is hard to see at night. The dogs were tracking a coon, and dad and Pink was trying to keep up with the hunt. They came to a fence and had to climb over it. Dad didn't know a black cow had bedded down next to the fence and it was too dark to see her. When he stepped off the fence he stepped right straddle the cows back. She came up snorting and bucking until she threw him off. Fortunately he was not hurt, but as you might guess he never lived it down. A few years later we moved from north of Rushville to west of Rushville. The farm was located near Crooked Creek and dad was still hunting. If the dogs didn't return to us in the woods they would always be home by morning. On one occasion dad was hunting near crooked creek with Buck. When he got up the next morning, Buck was not on the porch by his coat as expected. Dad called for him but there was no response. That was the last he ever saw of the dog he loved so much. For several days dad searched for Buck, but he finally had to accept the fact that he probably fell through the thin ice. My dad continued to hunt till his health began to fail, but it was never the same without Buck. Many years have passed since those events took place, but the memories like these are to be remembered and cherished.

THE RESCUE

By Donna Irwin Lerch

My name is Donna Irwin Lerch, and my dad was Bryon Pink Irwin, I look back on my dads coon hunting with fond memories. My dad loved to hunt, but it was a lot of work. He had to prepare the hides to sell. My most vivid memory of coon hunting was one cool calm night, my dad was standing on our porch and called for my mother Leila to come outside, of course I was right on her heals. Dad said "listen, I think I hear someone calling for help", my mom and I both said we didn't hear anything. Dad insisted he heard someone calling for help. He said he was afraid it might be our neighbor Vic Chockey. Vic had diabetes very bad. Dad told my mom to saddle up our horse and we would go ahead and when we found out who it was we would call out to her, so she could come to us. As we went deeper into the woods we became more anxious not knowing what we were going to find. We started to hear the voice more clearly, it was Vic's voice. He was yelling "help me please, help me", my dad was calling out to him "Vic, hang on we are coming", it was a long way from our house to where he was. He was on an adjoining farm and owned by Frank Yates. When we got to him, dad called his name. Vic started crying, and said "Oh Pink, I thought no one would ever find me". Vic said the dogs had treed a coon, and he had climbed the tree to shake the coon out and fell and broke his leg very badly. Dad said "Vic, I've got to go find someone to bring a pickup truck to get you out of here and to the hospital". We were lucky the tree he fell out of was in a clearing. Dad said to me "Donna you stay with Vic, I'll be back as soon as I can. I had known Vic and Esther since I was a little girl, Vic always called me Donnie! After dad left Vic said "Donnie, will you light me up a cigarette," I said "I have never lit a cigarette before in my life, but I will try". Dad had to walk a long way to find a truck but Frank Yates was at home. They brought back blankets and loaded Vic up. We took him to the hospital at Rushville. In all the excitement we forgot to call out to my mom. She had rode the horse into the woods, when she didn't hear us calling her she went back. We had someone call Esther, Vic's wife, she went by our house and told my mom where we were and she came and picked us up. Vic recovered fully from his injuries and lived many more years. I'm sure he told this story many times to family and friends until his death.

A OPOSSUM INSTEAD OF
A COON

By Donna Irwin Lerch

This is a story told to me by a good friend that used to live in Rushville area, Mary Ellen Marquis Beatty. Mary Ellen's dad was Russell Marquis, who was also a good friend of my dad, Pink Irwin. Mary Ellen said one night she went hunting with her dad Russell, they walked a long time when all at once the dogs treed what they thought was a coon. It turned out to be a possum! It was up a small bush. Russell reached up and got the possum. He laid it in the curve of his arm, Mary Ellen said she was so scared. She said "Oh dad, it will tear your arm to pieces" but the possum lay as still as could be and the dogs went on. Russell and Mary Ellen walked a ways farther, then Russell put the possum on the limb of a large bush, and they walked on. Mary Ellen said it seemed like miles, before the dogs treed a big coon. He had shot it out. She said they went home that night with just one big coon. Russell hunted every night that he could. He sold the hides for money for his family, just like my dad and many other families. Mary Ellen went with her dad many times, sometimes they were lucky enough to get three or four big coons. Mary Ellen said it was kinda fun then, but she wouldn't want to do it now.

COON HUNTING WITH A BAD HAND

By Jack Lerch

Back in November 1969, just before coon season, I cut my finger on a wizard knife at work. They took me to the hospital to sew it back in place.

I was more upset about the possibility of missing out on any hunting than about my accident and injured hand..

Luck was with me though, because the Dr. released me on November 15th, opening day! Against my wife's wishes and warnings, I rested all afternoon and as she was preparing our supper I started getting ready to head for the woods.

It was a cold and rainy night, but it was opening night and I had to go! I loaded up my dogs, Laddy Jack my beloved Old Black and Tan and Sarge a half Blue Tick and half Red Bone pup. I wrapped bread sacks around my bandaged hand and off I went. I hadn't been in the woods long when the dogs hit a hot track. It sounded like music, nothing like the sound of a dog on a hot trail. Heading towards them, I started wondering if after all this walking if I would be able to shoot my gun to get the coon. They were treed across what seems like the biggest holler.

It took me a bit but I finally found the coon on a limb about 20 feet up. The dogs were treeing hard, I finally found a way to hold my light under my arm. I was still having trouble seeing down the barrel of my gun. After about ten shots and still missing the coon, I found a limb with a fork just the right height to balance my gun, after about four more shots, I finally hit the coon!

While I was trying to get him from the dogs something fell out of the tree, hitting me on the back of the head. Lucky . . . . I shot two coons out of that tree!! I hadn't spotted that second one. By this time I was feeling poorly, my hand was hurting and I figured it was time to head home.

With two coons, my rifle, and my arm in a sling, I couldn't leash the dogs. I hoped they would follow me to the truck, which they did for awhile. Then smelling a scent off they went. I knew I better follow. I walked about a quarter of a mile to where they had treed. Shining my light into the tree it was a danged old possum! I managed to get the lead on my old dog and I knew the pup would follow, and we headed home at last.

BROKEN LEG

By Nancy Briggs Lung

One afternoon while visiting with Roy's family, his sister Ruth and husband Bob Carr from Warsaw, IL had came down and we were talking about coon hunting. Bob had broken his leg at the time and was in a cast from his hip down . . . he was an avid coon hunter and the season had just come in and he hadn't been able to go. He was called "Redbone" in Warsaw cause he hunted so much. We decided to take him and help him on the trip. So me, Ronnie and Roy Lung, Ronnie Hess and my brother Willie Briggs and I took Willie to get his gear to go hunting. Off we went . . . going up the first hill wasn't bad, then dogs treed across a big hollow. It was then we realized that crushed leaves dried leaves wasn't the best situation. But with great difficulty we got Bob down and up the steep hill on the other side. We were all worn out by this time, so when the dogs treed the next time we let Roy and Ronnie go to them and we waited on the ridge. Each fence we had to lift Bob over, and one barbed wire fence we held it up and rolled him under. We had 3 coons when we came to this corn field that had been picked and we thought we would cross it and walk to the woods on the other side and head towards home in a more level playing field. After two guys lifted Bob over the web fence with three barb wire on top and two guys on the other side we got him across. As we got half way across the field the dogs began to hang around our feet so badly we could not hardly walk. Ronnie turned his light on and seen nothing but eyes glowing back, he yelled "cows, turn out your lights and head for the fence", we all took off running and I remember Roy hitting me in the back and yelling "get over the fence!!!" The cows were stampeding behind us and breaking the corn stalks and they were so loud you couldn't hear anything. As I got to the fence, looking for the nearest fence post to get over the fence, my heart dropped as I thought about Bob, where was he, and had someone helped him. As we all got over the fence, our faces all got white as the cows knowing the fence was there ran up along it, then someone said "where is Bob ?" Willie was yelling "Bob, Bob, Bob" And from a tree about 10 feet from us was Bob. Bob answered with "what took you guys so long?" After that we decided to walk down the road and head back home. Bob took plenty of teasing going home. We asked him how he had beat us all to the fence and managed to get over the fence without all of us helping him. He told us he had learned with the encouragement of the cows behind him, he could swing his cast and get some momentum and could get a couple of steps and a huge stride..and by the time he got to the fence and the thought of disaster, he just pole-vaulted over the fence with his cast as a pole. As we got back home and drinking coffee and telling of our experience, Bob was setting on the couch and as we got up to go Bob asked for help getting off the couch, needless to say we all just laughed at him and told him not to play that helpless Bob to us . . . !

THE RACOON HUNT
By Bernard Marvel

I no longer raccoon hunt anymore, but I will always remember one night that I went hunting with a neighbor and long time friend Larry Egbert. We hunted together not only raccoons, but coyotes and deer. Raymond's son Larry was just about always by his dad's side when we hunted. We usually hunted here around the neighborhood because neither of us liked to stay out too late. I had a job selling feed and Raymond farmed so we would never go to far from home during the week nights. On occasion we would venture over to Rushville when we were invited by another long time friend, Charlie Houser to hunt there. This particular night we decided to hunt on a nearby farm close to Larry's house.

The hunt started about 6:00 pm. The dogs cast out and were soon tracking a pretty hot trail. After a few minutes the dogs were treeing solid and we worked our way around several ravines. We arrived at the tree and shot the raccoon for the dogs to finish the kill. The dogs left us and began to cast out again and we sat down on a trunk of a dead fallen tree and listened. It seamed they couldn't get another track started right away so Larry said "why don't we build a fire while we wait?" He had the fire going in just a few minutes and lo and behold he pulled out a pack of wieners out of one pocket and in his hunting coat and a pack of buns out of another pocket. We make some sticks and in no time we were roasting wienies. I asked if anyone had some ketchup, and out came a bottle of ketchup from Larry's coat pocket. Raymond and I looked at each other for a second and then we both busted out laughing. At that moment we both knew that Larry had planned this earlier. I don't remember much more about the rest of the night.

I think they were the best wieners I had ever eaten. Raymond and Larry and I had many other memorable hunts also and I will never forget them. I would like to dedicate this story to Raymond and Larry Egbert for their longtime friendship and being good neighbors'.

TO WINDY TO HUNT

By Bernard Marvel

One night Raymond Egbert and I made the trip to Rushville to hunt with a couple of long time friends and fellow hunters Charlie Houser and Harry Elliott. Charlie said that we could hunt on Bryon Ross's that night. We parked the trucks at Bryon's house and let the dogs out there. We hunted to the south of the buildings. The dogs cast out ahead of us and was silent for an hour or so. There were four dogs in all that was hunting and it was pretty strange that one of them hadn't struck a trail. It was very windy and it was decided to continue on south. Shortly we heard the dogs about a half mile away that we thought must be one of ours. We couldn't hear it for only short intermediate barks because of the wind. We got so far down in there that we weren't sure exactly where we were. I didn't know where we were, and it made me kinda uneasy that Charlie wasn't sure either.

As the time went on, we never heard the dogs at all. I think the wind was blowing even harder than when we started. Finally, we walked towards a pole light and got close enough to figure out our location. We were a long way from the truck and it was getting late. It was a week night and Raymond and I never liked to hunt late on those nights. We called and called and whistled for the dogs but they never showed up. I think all four of us made ourselves hoarse from calling so much. It was still very windy, we thought they might be back at the truck waiting on us so we made our way back to the truck, but there were no dogs there. We waited for about and hour thinking they would trail back to us which had happened on some earlier hunts. We called and whistled and waited. Finally we decided to go home without them. Charlie didn't live too far away and he thought his dog knew the way and would come home. We would leave the dog boxes for the other dogs and come back for them in the morning.

When I drove in the driveway about 11:30, our kitchen light was on, and that ment my wife was not in bed. When I walked in the door, she asked if I brought the dog home with me, and I asked her how she knew that I didn't have the dog? She said one of Bryon's neighbors had called about 7:30 and said he had them tied up at his house. They had come to his house when they had heard his dog barking at them. When I went the next morning to get my dog, the neighbor said he had fed them and wanted some money for the feed. It was agreed that $10.00 would be sufficient. I really didn't think my dog could eat $10.00 worth of food overnight, but maybe four dogs could!!

I guess because it was so windy the dogs didn't want to hunt very bad. Their collars always had our name and phone numbers on a small tag that was riveted to it. We were just glad to have our dogs back. We never hurt the raccoon population that night.

THE RUSHVILLE FFA COON HUNT

By Morris McClelland

The Rushville FFA Coon hunt began in the fall of 1970. I believe FFA Seniors Rick Powell, Frank Morrell and Jack Kelly, with the help of Dick Powell, Don Lerch, Dick Bowers and others from the Schuyler County Coon Hunters Club organized the first Rushville FFA Coon Hunt. The Schuyler County Coon Hunters always held their hunt on the opening night, which was usually November 15th. The FFA planned their hunt on the first Saturday after the opening day. Later we locked in our date to be the first Saturday after Thanksgiving.

Originally, the FFA hunt was for individuals with prizes awarded for the heaviest, 2nd heaviest and most hunted. Tickets were sold at the door the night of the hunt and you could hunt in groups if you wanted.

The FFA coon hunt also held a raffle along with the hunt and tickets were sold for $1.00. Most of the prizes awarded were donated items like dog food, oil changes, farm items and hunting supplies. The grand prize was usually a wheat light.

In the fall of 1974, I was hired to teach Agriculture at Rushville High School. Probably the first thing I was told, was how important the FFA coon hunt was. I think I heard it not once, but 100 times of how big of an event the FFA coon hunt was. In planning for the coon hunt, I talked to Don Lerch about some of the problems with the FFA coon hunt. It seemed that if hunters did not have a good night they would pool their coons and try to take the prize for the most coons hunted. This caused only a few hunters to buy tickets. Don proposed doing away with the prize for the most and instead award a "Lucky Weight" which was drawn at the end of the night.

After talking with the FFA members we decided to make the changes. Danny Hanning purposed to go a step further by hosting a "Buddy Hunt". He felt that everyone pretty much hunted in groups of two anyway, so we should establish that as our hunt. We set the buddy coon hunt tickets for $5.00 per two hunters, and others could tag along.

Our prize would be two trophies per winning group, one per buddy. We also established the "Lucky Weight" award.

Over the years, the Rushville FFA Buddy Coon Hunt has remained the same. We have always awarded the first and second place heavy coons and the Lucky Weight, which was decided by the drawing that night from all the coons turned in. We use to have a rule that required all coons be hunted legally by dogs.

It was amazing to me how competitive coon hunting was in the 70's around Rushville. I think the driving force was the price of coons. Raccoons were sold from $25.00 to $50.00 per pelt. It was very common for some people to invest thousands of dollars into coonhounds and hunting equipment. Several of the hunters attending our coon hunts were making a living out of raising and training coonhounds, plus hunting and trapping coons.

Because of the intensity of the raccoon business, the FFA was advised by many people how to make a more competitive and fair event.

Over the years very little has changed about the FFA coon hunt. That is the hunt itself. Probably the only thing that has changed was the type of raffle prizes. The first few years we offered a 22 Rifle and a wheat light plus other hunting supplies. We always had plenty of dog food donated from Don and Char Lerch and Schuyler Brown F.S. We usually had around 30 items total and always kept our raffle ticket price at $1.00 Later we made the Remington 870-12 gauge shotgun our grand prize and increased our prizes to around 50 items. The raffle became a main event by itself, even when guns became outlawed on school grounds. We just replaced the gun with a $300.00 grand prize. Even if we had a bad night for the hunt we always had a big turn out for the raffle. Of course you could not have a coon hunt without food and drink. We started in early years with just donuts, coffee, hot chocolate and soda. Over the years we expanded to popcorn, chips, subway sandwiches, and roast pork sandwiches. Some of our hunters, especially the young ones, the food was one of the most important thing.

When I look back over my 37 years of helping host this FFA coon hunt, it has amazed me how little it has changed, and then again how great the hunting of coons has changed. Our hunt has always cost $5.00 per buddy team and $1.00 per raffle ticket. We have always given away the same awards, but the hunting of coons has drastically changed. In the early years we had a lot of hunters who were very serious. Because the price of coon pelts dropper out to $5.00 to $15.00 per pelt, everybody has pretty well got out of the business. Today, if anyone is serious about hunting coons they have a good job to support the habit. In the early years we would have about 100 hunters turning in around 75 coons, while in the last 10 years we would have about 150 hunters turning in approximately 130 coons.

Over the years, the coon hunt had several surprises. However the early years we did have one event, it appeared we had 2 coons turned in that only had ½ pound difference in their winning weights. The guys who were second place threw a fit and demanded that we re-weigh, so we did, and in re-weighing a wheel weight fell out of the coons mouth. Needless to say they were embarrassed and they left the hunt—leaving everything, including their coons behind. For the most part, the hunters have always been a great group of people to work with.

All in all, the Rushville FFA Buddy Coon Hunt is a great event. The FFA Chapter has never used it as a money making event, but as a great hunting event.

LOOK UP IN THERE

By Dick Meehan

It was another full moon in December 1978. Raccoons were getting harder to tree now on the outside due to the winter settling in and of course that darn full moon. We gathered at my house on this particular night with the hope of treeing a big coon which is worth then right at $40.00 dollars. It would be a welcome sum to us high school kids who were trying to collect enough money to buy gas for our trucks and of course Christmas.

Myself and Jeff "Jeep" Althiser decided to give Dicky Fisher and Donnie Welker a call and go hunting tonight. I had my Plott hound named Babe, Jeep had his treeing walker "Sally" and Dicky and Donnie brought their locally famous English Red Tick named Lew.

Like previously stated, it was getting darn hard to tree a coon, and it was the main reason we gave a call to our two friends from Summum to see if we could get some help with their powerhouse hound. We had this particular spot where huge coon tracks were evident in this tributary creek located west of our house which leads down over the hill crossing the Fulton County, Schuyler County line into Schuyler County.

Little did out invited guests know, Jeep and I had cut loose there several times in the past couple of weeks and we had always ended up at this old railroad track bridge, which crosses Sugar Creek, and every time our dogs would get stumped at this bridge, just running around in circles with their heads in the air barking as maybe like saying in their bark "where did they go?". Well it was 7:00 pm and we loaded up the hounds and headed for the woods. We turned loose in this seemingly coon infested spot. Immediately Babe strikes a track then Sally and Lew join the race. It was another long race as was the last time we hunted there. The hounds were once again heading down the hill towards Sugar Creek and that dan gummed bridge. I looked at Jeep simultaneously as he sneered at me and we knew where the hounds would end up. As we walked in that direction, we decided to fess up to our invited coon hunters what had happened several times previous when we were here.

As we headed towards our hounds, it appeared they were hung up again at our familiar location.

As we approached we can see the outline of the huge train bridge in the glisten of the moonlight. We arrived with the similar results as our aforementioned hunts our hounds were once again flat out confused as we were. As we were catching our hounds and leashing them up, we decided to look at the situation over a little more closely.

We were once again fascinated at the size of the amount of iron in this ancient and seaming antique bridge. Looking at the bridge and the situation over, that coon sure put the slip on these hounds as we conferred with each other. Grabbing our hounds and thinking that coon just can't be caught we started leading our hounds back. Donnie turned back and looks at the old bridge one more time as we stop and splash our way away from the bridge when eyes were seen.

I looked at Donnie who said "I see eyes" and I asked him "where"? he said "look up in there". As we got closer to the bridge, my high power wheat light followed his four cell flashlight to the upper square beams of the bridge some twenty-five plus feet up. "Wow," I exclaimed as I shined the upper bridge beam. Glowing eyes were quickly scurrying to and fro in the hollowed beams. Now all kinds of thoughts were dancing in my mind. First of all I thought "so this is where all you little rascals have been giving our hounds the slip". Then I surmised, "There must be ten coons in this bridge," so our hounds have been running more than one coon every time they tracked them. Now I was extremely excited about our find, but one problem, how were we to get these coons!

As we were devising. Contemplating and collaborating, a sound of clanking and scuffing was heard. Much to our surprise, Donnie was already on top of those upper beams hanging upside down. I yelled at him "what the devil are you going to do now?" He said "I can get these coons out of here if you can shoot them first". So he climbed back down the beams to where we were as we began to shoot the glowing eyes in the beams of the bridge. Six raccoons were taken from the bridge as our part monkey friend pulled them through the holes of this old train bridge upside down.

Walking back to our truck with six large coons was too much so we decided to skin them critters out, which seemed like it took forever. As we arrived back at the truck we started dreaming of a big pay day for these furred up pelts. Guesses we made to how much we would receive.

The next day our coveted catch was taken to Rushville, Illinois to Don Lerch who was the fur buyer for the area. Oh what a payday for us broke youngsters. All to the help of our invited friends who said "look up there!"

NEW YEARS EVE MAGIC

By Clay Mitchell

I am starting my story of a very unique coon hunt by telling you how I was introduced to this great sport. My Grandfather W.T. (Breezy) Mitchell was a Bluetick coon hound lover his entire life and took me on my first coon hunt when I was about 10 years old. He said to me on one of our many hunts that you will have something different happen to you on every hunt that could make it memorable, he was right.

On New Years Eve 2005 I called Gary Welty, a friend of mine, that if he wasn't ringing in the News Years Eve at a party we could ring it in with a coon hunt. Needless to say Gary was all for the coon hunt. We drove to a beautiful tract of hardwoods on some neighbors in Brown County and got ready to turn the dogs loose. The night was cold and crisp with a million stars overhead. Gary had a fine Redtick named Sara; I had two blueticks named Margie and Sadie. We were always teasing each other about which of our dogs is better, the redticks or the blueticks as we turned them loose into the night. It wasn't to long before the dogs struck a track and trailed into a tree about a quarter mile away. The field edge crunched with frost as we trekked on across and into a grove of Hickory and Oak trees, finally arriving to the tree hoping Mr. Coon was up there. We were pleased that they had the coon and had done a really good job finishing the track. Over the next couple of hours we did tree another coon and felt fortunate as by this late in the season coons generally are very hard to tree. We decided to cut the dogs loose one more time and see if we could tree one more ringtail. About ten minutes passed when Sara hit a track, joined by Maggie and Sadie, the dogs warmed the track up really quickly and soon the unmistakable chopping barks of dogs treeing could be heard. The multi floral rose briars tore at our cloths as we soldiered on through a small clearing in a creek bottom and up a small hillside to get to the large Red Oak tree where the dogs were treed. When we arrived I commented to Gary the coon looked very light colored on its belly.

Well when it was time to get the coon out to dogs. When the dogs had finished the coon and we had a chance to look at it we totally amazed at what we saw! The coon was like any other normal coon except that she was almost entirely silver in color with only the faintest of rings on the tail. Needless to say I have talked to a lot of coon hunters who have never treed one quite like this one. The combination of New Year's Eve and our "Silver coon" made my Grandfather's words ring true that something can happen on any given hunt that can make it the most remarkable one.

CLIMBING THE TREE
By Dan Norvell

After a cool snap it warmed up a little and I unsnapped my old dog Sambo and picked up Gilbert Allen and his dog Duke, I don't remember where we went, but it was the tail end of the season and we were in Ridge Runner Territory. We hit a track and they ran a country mile or there about. They treed up a big ole Oak tree. I shot it and it fell and lodged about 30 ft up, so I told Gilbert I could get it, by climbing up the tree beside it and swing over to the Oak tree. I tried to get the coon but couldn't get it at night, so I had to get down. I was standing on a big limb and told Gilbert to shine his light over the tree about 6 ft from me, and I asked him if that was a Hickory and he said it was. Well at night you can't always tell if a limb is dead or alive! So I jumped and grabbed the tree limb. Well it was dead!! It held me till my body was parallel to the ground and then it broke! I fell about 15-18 feet on my back and butt. It was a steep hillside with lots of leaves and that's what the good Lord put there for me to land on. Anyway I ran a stick up my pant leg and of course the dogs thought I had the coon, I guess. I was trying to get this stick out of my pants and Gilbert thought it was my leg bone, and he said "Oh dang how bad did you break your leg," well I told him it was only a stick but I would have to break it to get it out of my pant leg. Gilbert felt better after that. We quit for the night after that but did go back the next day and got our coon.

GETTING EVEN

By Dan Norvell

It was a dark night and I picked up Phil Fitzgarrald, and we took off somewhere coon hunting. It wasn't long and the dogs hit a track and treed on a steep hillside. They had 3 coons up this big tree. We shot all 3 coons out, and of course they all fell down the steep hill as I recall it was real steep getting down there to them. Phil took one and I took the other and one was already up the hill. As we were climbing up, which was really difficult, we were grabbing any sprout we could for support to pull ourselves up. The coon I had was still kicking and I was busy grabbing and holding on to a tree to get me and the coon up the hill, and all of the sudden it felt like something bit inside my thigh, I thought the coon had bite me! I threw that sucker down the hill and grabbed my leg, then I saw Phil laughing at me and I knew he had pinched me on the inside of my leg. I then had to go back down the hillside and get the coon again!! I made sure Phil was not behind me.

Sometime later my son Brad caught a black snake and I told him if he saw Phil to throw it towards him. Well after about 3 tries it landed on Phil's shoulder, I didn't expect that to happen, but that's what getting even is all about!!

HUNT WITH A BOYFRIEND

By Carol Parker

My first time coon hunting was in 1981. I wasn't impressed with it at all. It was cold and all I had was a flashlight. My boy friend, Bob Parker, at that time whom later I married, had a nite light. It took quite awhile before we heard the dogs. We were hunting on my parents farm. The dogs only treed one time, and it was a false bark. We decided to call it a night. Mother nature called to my boy friend. He propped his gun on a fence post and then we continued to the house. We had been in about an hour and all the dogs but one came in. We had taken 3 dogs. The Black and Tan was a new one for Bob. When he didn't come in we got in the truck and went down the road. We saw the dog running down the road. He absolutely would not come to us. This went on for a couple of hours. The dog finally tired out and loaded up and we went home. The next morning Bob realized he had left his rifle leaning on the fence post. We went and got it. Sometime in the night someone had made a camp fire where Bob had left his gun, there were empty cans laying all around. Amazingly enough the gun was still there. I went on quite a few hunts but never did really like it. After a couple of years I quite going. Bob had many, many hunts in his lifetime. He quit hunting in 1999, when he was diagnosed with cancer and had to have his voice box removed. He is with the good Lord now. Maybe he has gotten some hunting done in heaven cause he loved to coon hunt. God Bless him.

THE PAPERS

By Dick Powell

Back in the 60's coon hunters started talking about seeing ads in books about coon dogs having papers and being registered. The more I heard about it the more I wanted a dog with papers. I would talk to other coon hunters that is about the registered dogs. Most remarks about that time was papers will not tree a coon.

One day I was talking to Paul Busby who had coon hunted all his life. I asked Paul what he thought about dogs being registered, and he said it would be ok. Then Paul looked at me and said "Dick, don't you have a dog that will tree a coon," and I said "yes, Paul I have a pretty good dog." and Paul said "well, what more do you want". He had a point! When I slowed down coon hunting in the 80's most everyone had registered dogs with papers and so did Paul Busby!!

COON HUNTING
WITH GOOD FRIENDS

By Dick Powell

In seventy years of hunting I have had lots of good times and made lots of good friends. Coon hunting as a small boy with my father, Gale Powell, he has carried me home if I got tired, but I enjoyed the hunt and dogs. I remember Virgil "Happy" Sours had an old dog named "Jigs". When we treed the first coon and shot it out Jigs would go home. As a boy about ten years old I would walk about 2 miles through the woods to George Turners and go coon hunting with him. About 1946 I had 2 good dogs "Buck" and "Red" at that time I only had dad's car to haul my dogs. Ernie Shanks and I went coon hunting, we had hunted every night that season. The dogs were tired so we would hunt Buck till midnight and put him in the car and turn Red loose. Instead of putting Buck in the trunk as usual we put him in the back seat, when we got back to the car about 3:00 am, Buck had torn about all the upholstery out of the inside of the car. I also remember the night Les Redshaw, Ralph Knowles and attorney Ernie Utter (everyone called him Pete) and I went hunting. Pete always wore a suit, no tie but a top coat. When we got back Pete had torn the bottom of his top coat and it looked like he had on a jacket. Don Fagan and I had been talking about quitting smoking, so one night Don and I went hunting and Don says "Dick, I quit smoking and I am now chewing!" Later that night he swallowed that chew and turned green, and was terrible sick, needless to say we didn't hunt long that night. Breeze Mitchell, Lloyd Reische, Don Fagan and I went hunting on mules. One night as we were crossing a creek, Breeze's mule got tangled up in a grape vine. Breeze fell off and the mule took off. We hunted for the mule about 2 hours and couldn't find him. The next morning the mule was in the pasture at home which was about 2 miles, the saddle was hanging under the mule and bridle and reins torn up. We were a mule short coming home but it was a good night and I got to spent it with good friends.

THE BOBCAT

By Jared Prather

In the fall of 2011 Tyler Rensch and I was coon hunting, he had two walkers hounds named "Money and Maggie" and I had an English hound named Penny. It was mid November, the weather was clear and it was warm for that time of the year. We were hunting near Camden and we were treeing coons one after another and we had multiple coons in almost every tree, so we decided to hunt all night. We made our next dump at Dale Wells house a little after midnight. The dogs took off on a track and headed Northwest. My dog and Tyler's dog Money treed in a big den tree along the Lamoine River. So we caught up with them and Tyler's other dog was treed way off further to the north. We started walking to her. The moon was out just enough you could see in front of you to walk so we didn't have our lights on. When we got about 150-200 yards from her we kicked our lights back on to see where we needed to head and then the dog stopped treeing and fell treed further north. We stopped and waited this time thinking we had maybe rushed her. So we headed to her with our lights off and again when we got close we kicked them back on and she did it again. This happen multiple times and we were both wondering what was going on. We walked through big creeks with steep tall banks, through nothing but CRP. We finally got her caught north of Highway right beside Brooklyn. She finally did tree and had a coon.

So we agreed that the only explanation for her doing that was she was running a bobcat since this dog was hard going and never ever ran any trash at all. Then about a month later we were hunting in that same area and the dogs treed and something let out a sound that I have never heard before and then started fighting with the dogs. There was a silence, but they treed again in a big den tree over this big rock ledge. So I believe 100 percent that we treed two bobcats this year while coon hunting.

HUNTING THE GOOD OLE DAYS

By Kevin Price

Back in my younger years when times were simpler, and all we could think about was getting to the weekend so we could go coon hunting. Back then it was just a matter of stopping at a farm and asking the old feller if you could go hunting. More times than not it was "sure, hunt whatever you want and whenever you want". Not like now days. It didn't hurt that my dad sang country music and was an auctioneer. It seemed to me that he knew the whole country.

So, we would put a couple of dogs in the old dog box, pick up my Uncle Bob and cousin Shane and we were off. Don't get me wrong we were not hard cord coon hunters. Our hunts usually consisted of pulling into a place, dropping the tailgate and letting them go. Then we would sit on the tailgate, eating peanuts in the shell, ring bologna and drinking soda. The elders might have a beverage or two. That was that. We would sit and listen for the open, then we would make our way to the dogs. That's when the excitement usually started. You see our dogs were not what you would call stellar. Sometimes it was a coon sometimes a possum and even a few stray cats had been treed by old Luke. Sometimes he would lead you astray. But we were there for the fun and friendship anyway, getting a coon was a bonus I guess you could say. We always had fun. If we were lucky enough to get a coon we would be on the next night or the weekend. Back then a coon would fetch $15.00 to $25.00 dollars, depending on its size. Just enough for gas and goods the next hunt.

On occasion, my uncle Dave would go with us. He was serious about coon hunting. I believe he had a grand champion dog at that time. When we went with Dave, the tailgate dropped the bullshit stopped also. You better be ready to stay with the dogs all night long and be able to skin a coon damn near on the move. But we still had fun. We were certain to come home with plenty of pelts on those nights. On special occasions we would go over to the Schuyler County Coon Hunters Club for a club hunt. These were always good times. Getting to see all the other hunters. You always drew out in groups and went hunting. There would be a treeing contest at the club on these nights. Our old dog Luke might not have been the better hunter but man that dog could tree. More than one time he brought home a trophy. After the hunt, I remember waiting for everyone to get in to see their coons and tell their stories. You could always count on Hound Dog (Dick Bowers) to have some good chili and other eats ready.

A GOOD NIGHT COON HUNTIN'

IN SCHUYLER COUNTY

By Brian Ralston

I never liked coon huntin' all that much, but if I could go again with two of the guys I hunted with in the early to mid 1960's, I would go in a second. My brother Gary Ralston and his good friend Glenn Tillitt were both avid coon hunters and they took me along for shits and giggles and for my ability to pack out the coons they would track down while running the dogs. Once in a while they would say "Brian, can you shoot them out?", or Glenn would say "Come on Gary, give the kid a break and let him shoot this one." Well the night I remember the most was one of those kinds of nights. Glenn and Gary's dog had already treed four big coons that I was packing. So they said the next coon we got in the light I could shoot out. But before I got my chance, Glenn did something I never saw anyone do before and I'm sure I'll never see again. First he set me up for a joke. Glenn said "come here Brian, I want to show you something". So I walked up to where he was standing with my brother Gary who was about 10 to 12 feet off to his side and part of the joke they were about to pull on me, they set me up to walk right through a covey of quail bunched under some bushes, Glenn had spotted with his light. Stepping on a covey of quail in the dark is an experience that everyone packing 4 coons should have at least once in a lifetime. Well, Glenn and Gary laughed, and laughed for several minutes and the while I am cussing them out! I thought the joke was over till Glenn said "come over hear and help me find my hat." So I walked over to Glenn where he was bent down looking for his hat on the ground. When I got there he said he had just found it and glad because it was a new hat and had got it as a gift. When Glenn Said "Brian do you want to see it?", I said "sure". So he handed me the hat, I took it turned it over and out flew one of the quail! They had made me the butt of their jokes twice in a matter of 5 minutes or less and I still had not shot a coon. When the laughing stopped we went on hunting. The dogs had treed about 50-75 yards off to our left so away we went. Gary said he was sure the dogs were just up ahead and Glenn had said he had seen eyes just 10 feet off the ground or so we thought. I got ready to shoot the coon and Gary walked towards the sound of the dogs. That was until we heard Gary say "ooooh shit" and then thud while he was falling off the side of a hill and rolled down to where the dogs were. Gary was scratched up and bruised from top to bottom, but ok. This time me and Glenn got the laughs. We killed two more coons out of that tree and called it a night. On the way back to town that night, Gary and I were real quiet while Glenn kept saying "you Ralston boys are sure fun to hunt with, Brian how come you didn't catch that quail I handed you? Gary you got to watch where you are going and be more careful, yes sir, you Ralston boys sure are fun to hunt with!" I sure miss them both, they taught me a lot about life and about having fun. I wish I could be half the man either one of them was.

THE POSSUM
By Tony Reische

Never brag on your dog. That was a lesson I learned also at young age. Having just got my first coon dog I was looking for anyone that would put up with me and also my young and dumb mountain cur coon hound. My dad called a fellow from Rushville and he said he would come over with his old blue dog that was not very fast but one heck of an old dog for training young pups. So we picked a night and we met up. While talking about each others dogs and everything, he had mentioned about how his dog would run a possum for just a bit but would always break off. Again trying to teach me some hunting skills about good and bad dogs we decided it was ok as long as they would not make a habit of it. This night we were going for just a short hunt so we let the dogs loose and it was not very long before his old blue dog started barking a bit but nothing ever materialized too much. That was just enough to get that cur interested in barking and such, but none of us was ready for what was about to happen. About two thirds of the way through the hunt it looked like it was going to be another learning experience for the young guns again. We could see in our wheat lights something was coming at us. He said "that looks like ole Blue comin' at us"! and yip he was right it was his old dog with something in his mouth. The old dog came right up to him just like a Labrador retriever and dropped a big ole possum and turned around just like he had done it before. I looked at him and just started laughing, "I thought you said he would not even tough a possum let alone fetch one back for you" I said, with a startled look on his face and still to this day he swears that was the only time that dog of his had done that. Kinda hard to believe that, but then again an auctioneer wouldn't tell a lie would he???

OPENING NIGHT

By Tony Reische

Opening night of coon season, that is what you looked forward to when you are in your young teenage years but not old enough to drive to town legally yet. You could always find a neighbor that was going hunting and was willing to take you or so it seemed. This one in particular opening night it was going to be a bit cold out for the opener and all participants' was going to bring a sipping bottle with them to take the edge off the cold and frigid night air. It just so happened I had a bottle for such an occasion, peppermint schnapps was the flavor I thought was the only thing at that time. You could not beat that smooth and very cool yet warming sensation you received going down the gullet. As always we had a meeting spot and a time to gather at so we could discuss and prepare for the big hunt that was before us. Loading the dogs was always a theatrical moment in itself. Everyone of them had to smell each other, do a little growling and soon they were all getting along or out came the chain lead and there was not to many that did not know what that meant and they respected the old dog lead for the most part. So after getting the dogs loaded and everything off to what we thought was the best place for the night to bring in the biggest coon for the night at the weigh in. This particular night we headed to Versailles Township. The wind was blowing so we decided to hunt deep in the hollers for the evening. As we were driving we saw several coons crossing the road but never could time it just right to have a good start of the season without letting the dogs out of the box. Getting to our destination, we loaded up with snacks, ammo and sippin' bottles. This particular hunt I opted out of taking a gun because we had one of the best with us for shooting coons out of big tall trees, and that was sure going to be what we had tonight. Hunting with me tonight was the local legend commonly known as Golly. I cannot remember who else was there but quite a few of us. After letting the dogs go and trying to get them to go the way you wanted to hunt was a chore itself. The dogs were very rowdy after being cooped up all year. We proceeded to hunt down this long neck which had been in the corn that year and was hoping to make a big swing and come back around to the truck in a few hours. After having some decent luck and a lot of den trees we came across this ole tree that we knew had to have the winner in it, or so we thought. The dogs were in top form, after looking for a few minutes and working the dogs, ole Golly yelled out "I see him boys" for Golly to get a good shot he needed to climb to the top of the ridge, I stayed at the bottom to help with the dogs and hopefully not to let it get in the creek below. When the shooting began I thought maybe I should have at least brought some ammo along. After doing some trash talking about the shooting, I was told that he was just going to drop that ole coon on my head. Well not even knowing the angle of which the varmint would fall and all this I blurted out "not a chance in hell are you that good!" With that being said the next few minutes was words I just ate! You could hear the shots, but that old coon wouldn't give up. Finally I heard Golly say "here he comes boys, look out below" and just about that time I looked up and this huge fur ball coming at me. I turned and tried to get out of the path, forgot about the water, the dogs, all I was thinking about was getting out of the way. For the most part he had missed me except on the right side kidney area. I thought for sure the way he felt it had to be the one we were looking for. After getting the dogs and everybody gathered up we decided it was time for the sippin' bottles to be opened up before we marched out of the bottom and to the truck. All this time my right lower back had been burning and tingling. I ask Golly to get the bottle out of my back pocket and he started laughing, he had not only hit me with the coon, it had broken my bottle of Schnapps in my pocket. Golly was pulling the broken glass out of my pocket, I guess we know now what all the burning and tingling sensation was not the smooth and refreshing feeling that I knew and loved at the age with peppermint. The night was one to remember.

COON HUNTING "TAILS" I REMEMBER

By Lester Robertson

I started coon hunting at age 12 with a pup named "Rex" who was ½ Sheppard and ½ Bull Dog and a chicken killer. He became a excellent squirrel and ground hog hunter. One fall I took Rex out with a neighbors coon dog and he learned to tree coons. Then one night in 1942, after Dr. Corman left from treating my brother, Lyle who had the flu, Dad suggested he and I go coon hunting for awhile. Rex treed a coon about mile and half from home. The coon got to heavy so we skinned it. The coon measured 36 inches from hose to tail. My dad took the pelt to Rushville to John Spates who was a pelt buyer and John gave him $7.00 dollars. The other coon pelts were bringing $2.00-$3.00 dollars. John said it was the largest coon pelt he had ever bought. Most of my coon hunting was done with Raymond Egbert who had a Bluetick hound and by then I had a Black and Tan hound and a young Red Bone pup. One fall Raymond and I hunted (as I remember) every night of the season. One night at 10 degrees above zero (like fools) we went to Don Egberts hunting and we did get a coon. One night when Raymond came over we picked up Bernard Marvel who wanted to go with us. Raymond who was a practical joker, I decided to have a little fun. I had a couple of handy wipes (from some restaurant) and told Bernard that if we got a coon (which we did) we would have some fun. Bernard and I proceeded to skin the coon and no branch near to wash our hands, I took out of my pocket and gave one to Bernard and we proceeded to wipe our hands. Raymond was standing there watching, never saying a word. When we were done he turned and said "you d ____ panty waste" and stomped off. We had a good laugh.

Another time I remember we went hunting with an old man that had a "cold nose" dog. His dog hit a coon and bellowed and howled for several hours and finally treed. The old man said "there's a coon there, he never lies". When we finally got to the tree it was a big oak, we looked and looked with what light we had, but couldn't find anything. The dogs owner said he knows there's a coon up there, the dog never lies . . . there was a big fork in the tree and luckily I was able to climb up there and sure enough there was a pile of coon bones in the fork of the tree.. He sure was a "cold tracker". I have many memories of coon hunting with my dad and Raymond in the 40's and 50's. Two years in the 50's pelts would bring $40.00 a piece and we thought we were in hog heaven . . .

My dad and Raymond, both have passed on, I still remember and cherish those nights following our dogs . . .

HUNTING WITH FAMILY

By Mary Root

My name is Mary and yes as you might guess I loved to coon hunt. People can't believe that women would get out and walk the woods at night following dogs. But with me it was a passion. Out there on a cool crisp night listening to your dogs run, can't get any better than that. I always like to hunt, squirrel, rabbits, deer but mainly coons. In a little town like Industry we heard there was a man there that had a coon dog that he wanted to sell, we took him out on a test hunt, liked him so well that I bought him that night, he was a big treeing walker dog by the name of Sport. He was a long range hunter, he could take a cold track and, he had a short chop voice on track and a long bawl on tree that had to be the prettiest sound in the world to hear. My dad Carl Lashbrook is the one who got me started hunting he always hunted, and hunted as long as I can remember when we kids at home he would load us all up and off we would go to field trials and let his dog run. He always hunted by himself, mom would worry about him until he got home. One night he called and wanted to know if I wanted to go hunting, he had a black and tan named Hawk, he was a good coon dog, dad would say he was a old mans dog, always hunted close, didn't range out much. Anyway he came over and we loaded up the dogs and off we went. We went hunting at a place he use to live. As soon as we let them out of the box they took off, it wasn't long till dad's dog Hawk started to track and Sport chimed in with him. They took to hunting together like peas in a pod which made us both happy, they tracked for awhile and Hawk started treeing, then Sport started treeing with him, by the time we got to the tree they were both pretty set that the old coon was up there, and sure enough he was, a big ole coon in the top of the tree. Dad shot him out and he fell, he still had some life in him to give to the dogs and a pretty good fight, Hawk went for the throat and my dog went for the hind quarters, knowing he won't bite that way, after awhile we pulled the dogs off and told them to find another coon, they must have understood me because that's what they did. I pulled out the twine and slipped one end over the coons head and the other over his hind leg. It wasn't long before the dogs hit another track and warmed it up to where they started treeing again, this time they had two coons up the same tree. Dad said he had to shoot the first coon out dead or we might loose the second coon, because the dogs would be to busy with the first one to even notice the second one. Three coons and the night was still young so we gathered the dogs and off we went. Towards the sixth coon they were getting pretty heavy, something else was happening I got to having this funny feeling something was crawling all over my body. I told dad that these coons had fleas and that they were on me: he just laughed and shrugged it off. They got so bad that I couldn't carry them anymore so we had to stop and dad skinned them out. Which made them easier to carry and the fleas must have jumped off because they stopped crawling on me, what a relief that was.

After six coons and a load of fleas we called it a night. Dad and I went another night just the two of us and the dogs. It was kinda unfamiliar territory, I remember we walked by this tree and commented that it was a bear tree, see all the bear claw marks on it. When you hunt with your dad he never admits that he might be lost. He said he always knows where he is at, but we went by this tree three times. I asked him if he was lost and showed him the tree with the claw marks on it, and he just laughed and said he wasn't lost just wanted to see if I was paying attention to where we were at. We would go into some pretty steep hollers and climb up and down many hills I couldn't find my way out if I had to, wherever the dogs were treeing is where we went. One night we went out it was a poor night, we couldn't tree a coon for nothing, but there were other tree game. Sport treed 3 possums in a row and Hawk didn't tree with him, so we knew it couldn't be a coon, I got mad at him but Dad said not to scold him it was tree game, at least he was hunting. I really enjoyed coon hunting and visiting with my dad, listening to the dogs running and treeing, watching them fight the coons. Sure the money was good, but we went for the enjoyment of it. Some nights we got skunked but the dogs got their exercise and we did to. Some nights I would take my two sons Keith Jr and Brian, but I didn't take them on school nights just weekends. One windy night the coon was at the very top of the tree and the tree was swaying, Jr wanted to shoot it out and after a few shots the coon finally fell, we were pretty impressed. The more we hunted together the more they enjoyed it. Some nights we would go out and the dogs would not come in with us, so I would just throw my coat down on the ground where we let out, and sure enough the next morning they would be there laying on it. They were just as happy to see us as we were to see them. Another time we were hunting and dad shot this coon out and I was trying to encourage the dogs on, not paying attention to were I was standing and I fell into the creek with the coon and the dogs, just got lucky it was a mild night and not real cold.

On another night I was packing a coon on my shoulder and it wasn't quite dead and it didn't take me long to shed that coon.

On another occasion dad and I went out with the dogs and they were doing their thing and we ran into a pack of coyotes, boy that was pretty scary, it didn't take the dogs long to come back to us, dad just said to back up to this big tree and have your gun ready, they must have lost interest in us, before long they left except one, and she kept baying at us but after awhile she quit. The dogs finally started to wonder off and started hunting. There was another time when we were hunting and dad shot this coon out and the dogs were there to fight but the coon had other thoughts about that. Dad evidently missed because that coon climbed right down that tree and faced then dogs, he gave them a good fight and walked off and do you think them dogs could figure out where he went, no way!! Dad said that sometimes the track is to hot and the dogs cant pick it up. Well I don't coon hunt anymore but I still deer hunt, sometimes I think I would like to but I am older and don't move as good as I use to. Both dad and my dogs are in heaven now probably chasing coons all night long up there, but these had to be the best times of my life, and I will cherish these memories forever.

CLUB HUNT

By Jim Robeson

I went on a club hunt with Wendell Stritzel and Charlie Hendricks. We went to sugar creek bottoms where there was a lot of standing corn and it was about 100 degrees. Charlie had a walker named "Rebel", and Wendell had a blue tick named "Drive" and I had "Daisy Mae". We turned them loose and they all hit the track, each one came back and forth tracking about five times and finally all settled on the tree. It really turned out to be funny because there was five coons in the tree. The dogs were so hot when we got the coons out they got in the creek to cool off, what a great sport and lots of memories made and great people I met.

SIXTY YEARS AGO

By Kermit Schramm

Over 60 years ago, a buddy of mine and I were talking about how we used to go coon hunting with our dads when we were just kids. Naturally our wives picked up on the conversation and began questioning us about it. Well, we spread it on pretty thick about how much fun it was and how we wouldn't mind doing it again sometime. Then we brought up the subject of snipe hunting. That even made their interest higher. Eventually the girls decided they would like to try coon hunting. We said we would take them when the time was right and we set a Saturday night date for two or three weeks later. They even said they would like to go snipe hunting but we said we could do that after the coon hunt.

So, one dark drizzly Saturday night armed with a couple of flashlights and a .22 rifle we went to the woods in Woodstock township where I spent all my growing up years, and where I knew we would not get lost. After stumbling around the woods and listening to grips about the brush and wet bushes we actually did discover a coon in a tree strictly by accident by shining flashlights into the trees. We did shoot the coon and had to finish him off with a club. Then we heard how cruel it was to kill such a pretty animal and that we should be ashamed of ourselves. They said it was time to go home and we said okay. We had to cross a small creek by stepping on stones and in the process of crossing one of the girls missed a stone and stepped off into a foot of water. That made matters worse so we got out of there as quick as we could and back home where they found dry cloths and warmer temperatures. That ended all of our coon hunting days forever. Incidentally, we never did take them snipe hunting.

HUNTING WITH GRANDPA

By Allen Settles

When I was 6 or 7 my grandpa Etter took me coon hunting. He raised hogs and the hog lot was about ¼ mile from the house next to the woods. Anyway grandpa asked me one night if I wanted to go coon hunting with him and of course I said "sure". We waited till about 10:00 pm and away we went. I remember grandpa and I had two 6 volt battery flash lights and a 410 double barrel shotgun with duck tape holding it together. Grandpa had 2 dogs, a blue tick and a Chocolate Labrador. The Chocolate Lab was better than most coon hounds, the only problem being, you didn't know when he had a coon because he didn't bark!. Anyway it was a lot of fun for a young boy from town. I don't remember ever shooting any coons, but I sure had a good time with grandpa.

BISHOP SPRINGS HOLLER
By Don Shaw

I hadn't been coon hunting very long when Sam Gust and I went to one of his spots. It wasn't to far from his house and had coons aplenty. We had treed and got an easy coon when the dogs treed at the edge of the timber, we got to the dogs and shot the coon out and it got drug clear to the bottom of the hill. After sliding down the hill to get the coon, Sam yells and said to come back up the hill. After pulling myself from tree to tree and dragging the coon back up the hill, Sam was sitting on a big log waiting for me. When I finally got my wind back Sam said he was going to call it a night. I ask which way was the best way to the truck, and he said "back down the hill you just came up." I told him that the hill was to steep and slick with leaves for him to try and make it down. He said that was alright that we would just walk about 25 yards around the point and we would walk down a logging road, he forgot to tell me about it until I was almost up to the top on my climb back up the hill. We made it back down the hill and walked the road back to the truck and headed home. We never went back there again, as far as I know the coons are dying of old age in "Bishop Springs Holler".

DOG IN A HOLE

By Joe Simpson

One night late November, Brent Clayton called and wanted to go coon hunting. His dad had gone down south somewhere and got him a coon dog and he wanted to try him out. We had treed several coons when the dog decided to go a long distance from where we were . . . we thought!

We continued to follow his barking and that's when we found he had not gone far, but had fallen into a brush pile the owner had bulldozed off. He was down about 10 feet and wouldn't come out. The only way he could get him out was to climb down and get him out, which I did. Guess what? That ended the hunting for the night.

COON IN A LOG

By Joe Simpson

Chuck Clayton and I went coon hunting one night and the dog treed up a small tree and when we shined the light on him he bailed out. The dog realized the coon had bailed and started tracking him.

Chuck and I sat on a log to wait for the dog to tree again. After a while the dog came back and started running from one end of the log to the other barking and barking. I said to Chuck "do you think that coon could be in this log?" We got up and started shining the log and sure enough there was the coon!

THE HUNTS OF GREAT COON DOGS

By Steve Skiles

Back in the 70's coon hunting became a sport that I became interested in. Of course growing up in the country and being around some of the old time coon hunters probably had something to do with it. I had an uncle, 2 cousins and my older brother Gail Skiles that were hunters. This probably contributed to my interest hunting with hounds. I remember the first dog I actually bought was and older silent trailer that was pretty good dog. His mane was Nipper, aptly named; because sometimes you would be walking through the woods, and he would come up and take your hand in his mouth never biting hard. He was not a pure breed dog, but a good dog none the less. He was an accurate tree dog, but I remember one moonlight night he treed and when I got to him all I could find was a hornets nest. I guess he couldn't find a coon that night. He didn't like riding in the back of the truck, he would rather ride in the front seat, which was ok until he swam in the creek or rolled in something dead. After hunting this dog for one winter I decided that would like to have an open dog. After looking around for awhile I found a man that had a litter of walker pups. I bought 2 female pups thinking I would train the two and pick out the best to keep. I hunted and trained these pups all summer and decided to keep the one that I thought was doing the best. The other one I sold to a man in Astoria and she turned out to be a good dog. The one I kept was a good honest strike dog but was not an overpowering tree dog. In her later years she did improve and would tree with dogs still running around her. As a young dog she like to tree possums, but as old Breeze Mitchell always said . . . it was easier to lead them off a tree than to lead them to a tree. I was a member of the Schuyler County Coon Hunters for several years during its day where I met several of the old time hunters and hunted in the summer club hunts. The above mentioned female "Molly" was high scoring female in about 1984 if my memory serves me right. I went on to own several walker hounds, one came from a well known hound man, John Wick from Missouri. I bought a walker female from a man in Warsaw, IL. She was about a year old and he didn't seem to have much of a story, so I thought she was worth a chance. She would go out hunting with the other dogs but didn't impress me much. On about the fourth or fifth night I heard a strange sounding dog treeing and when I arrived at the tree there she was stretched out upon the tree barking about 100+ barks a minute. That was the start of her good but short career. In the summer of the fourth year I came home from work to find her lying dead on her chain. I suspected that her stomach had twisted. The great ones always seem to die young. She was by far the best dog I ever owned. Now that many years have passed the hills have gotten steeper, the races longer, and the legs and hearing have given out. I have now gone to the Black Mouthed Cur Dog. I still like coon hunting, but like a lot of us old age limits my hunts. I do have a Black Mouthed Cur that is a good tree dog on squirrel, coon and possum. I like the Cur dog because they handle easy and are good companions. May all your hunts end at the tree fellow hunters. May this coon hunting tradition continue.

THE COON HUNT THAT ENDED IN A DOG HUNT

By Bill Smith

Dale Smith, Gene Stambaugh and I went coon hunting one night in Ray. I had two dogs a Red tick and a Blue tick. My dad and Gene had a walker dog. The walker dog started running a deer so I caught my dogs, we drove all over trying to catch him but could not until three days later we found him at Carl Skiles house near Browning, needless to say we didn't catch any coons that night.

A COON HUNT BY THE FIRE
By Bill Smith

Charlie Houser, Jim Henninger and I went coon hunting one night and the dogs would not hunt. After a while Jim said "I am going to start a fire" we sat there for three or four hours telling stories. Charlie said "we need some hot dogs" which none of us had. The dogs eventually came back to where we were and we leashed them and decided to head for the house.

A CAR FOR COON HUNTING

By Bill Smith

I didn't have a truck, but I had a old nineteen sixty Chevy car that served as a truck. I kept my newer car for work. My wife Stella and the kids would take the old car to the grocery store and to the Laundromat. They parked by someone at the store and a little boy said "look mom they have fence in their car", when I came home my wife was mad as a wild woman. She said she would not ever drive that car again, so from that day on I had to drive the old coon hunting car to work.

COULD NOT CARRY THE COON
By Jimmy Surratt

When I was 10 years old my dad and his two cousins took me coon hunting. In the big timber you slide down the big hills on your butt and crawl up the big hills. We had walker hounds, so we went hunting and treed a big coon in a big white oak tree that leaned way out over the creek. It took a bit before they shot the coon out. When they shot him he fell, landing in the creek bed, but it wasn't dead, and all three dogs were fighting it. They sent me down to get it and told me it was dead, boy was they wrong! I thought it was going to bite me after I got the dogs off it. I was pulling dog after dog out of the way so they wouldn't rip it up. After I got the dogs out of the way the coon was just about gone. I couldn't even pick it up and carry it up the hill. My dad came down and got it. I bet that coon weighed 30 lbs. We got three coons that night, and they were all big ones. We haven't gotten coons that big for a long time. These are times I will remember always.

BAD SHOTS

By Jimmy Surratt

One night I went coon hunting with my brother and buddy. We took dads walker and his pup, half walker and half pit bull. When you go hunting with my brother you take your own gun cause he will shoot a lot and not hit the coon. We started out real good, treed the coons up a small tree, they appeared to be small coons. I told my brother to shoot one out. But not kill it so the dogs could have some fun. Well he shot two coons out dead! I shot the last one out alive, I shot his bottom jaw and he came down that tree mad, just what I wanted for the young pup, she was nine months old, and she liked that. The two dogs killed that coon. When we got them going again, they treed a coon in a locus tree, way up high, my brother started shooting. I am on one side of the tree and they were on the other side, I bet they shot twenty times before I even seen him, by that time he was coming down the tree, mad, he wasn't hit he was just tired of being shot at. I raised my gun, started shooting at him and missed twice, then the third time I hit him. He came down and the fight was on. That pup grabbed him by the rear and he climbed on her, and with the help from the other dogs, they got the coon off, the pup tried to run away, but I grabbed her and threw her back into the coon. She fought with the coon better, she grabbed its head and bit down and it was over, she had killed it. When we got it away from her, we discovered it was a big coon, probably 25 lbs, but only one bullet hole!! We called it a night and went home with a nice bunch of coons for one night.

COON IN A BOAT

By Jeremy Taylor
Brown County Hound Supply

It was a still, dark December night. The kind of night every coon hunter gets excited about. Myself and Clay Mitchell couldn't get the dogs loaded in the truck quite quick enough. Clay was taking his female blue tick "Sadie" and I had my male red tick "Clyde". Our hunt this night took us just off Scotts Mill Road in the southern part of Schuyler County. With me living in Brown County, a mile from Schuyler County line, a lot of my hunting buddies are long time Schuyler County boys. Clay and I couldn't wait to turn the dogs loose and load the guns. We were not disappointed, it wasn't long till the dogs were stuck in on a good track and treed down on the creek. We had no doubt the way the dogs came on to the tree, that their would be a coon in it. We tied our dogs on down the creek and shined the tree and Clay shot him out. We sent the dogs on down the creek; after the dogs got the reward of chewing on the coon a bit. After a short while the dogs hit another track, giving us a chance to skin the coon and talk a little about how the dogs did on the first one. Clay's dog Sadie is a nice pleasure hound and done a good job when you took her. My dog Clyde was three years old at the time and the best dog I ever had the pleasure of owning. We were about three hours into the hunt and had treed several coons, but you could tell the hunt was coming to an end as the tracks were drying up. Clay and I had walked a good ways and were ready for a break. Sadie was down the hill trying to get something started, we were sitting on a pond bank in the clearing catching our breath. Clay asked where Clyde was and I told him that he was to our left in the timber. The tracks were cold and the dogs just couldn't get anything started. Clyde came out of the timber close to us with his nose still to the ground, he went up on the pond bank and to our left and was running back and forth with an excited squeal in his throat. As Clay and I sat on the pond bank talking about how nice of a hunt we had, Clyde came running by us headed to the far side of the pond. All of a sudden with no warning Clyde started treeing. It was to dark to see across the pond and with Clay knowing the ground we were hunting on, I ask him what kind of tree was on the other side of the pond. He said there were no trees over there and had no idea what Clyde would be treeing on, so it was time to go see. As we came around the pond we found Clyde barking and digging at a jon boat that was flipped over on the bank. Clay scratched his head and giggled a bit and ask what my dog was doing. I looked at Clay and told him there must be a coon under the boat; Clay laughed and said "no Way". Well there was only one way to find out, so I grabbed the boat and flipped it over. Sure enough, there he was, back up to the transom of the boat with nowhere to hide. Clyde rushed in, grabbed the coon and the fight was on. They ended up in the pond fighting it out and all we could do was watch. Clyde ended up killing the coon in the water and brought it back out onto the pond bank with him. I was very proud of my dog and somewhat relieved that he didn't get hurt fighting that coon in open water. I have seen that kind of thing go bad before.

We skinned the coon, put Clyde on a lead and headed down the hill to catch Clay's dog, having all the excitement we could handle for one night. After making it back to the truck we took a minute to laugh about treeing a coon in a boat, we should have had a camera to take pictures. To this day, when Clay and I hunt together the story of Clyde and the boat is still something we talk and laugh about. Its hard to be a coon hunter and not have stories to tell, it's just some stories are closer to your heart than others.

FORGOT THE GUN

By Steve and Harlin Terry

Dad recalls that one night he and his son-in-law, Harold Hood went coon hunting. They probably walked a mile or so and the dogs treed a coon. One ask the other to shoot it, well neither one had brought a gun, so they turned around and walked back to the house to get it, then back to the coon and shot it. I'm sure the next time they went they remembered the gun, shells, etc.

Through many years there were many people that hunted with dad, Alvin Hamilton, The Forman's and just about whoever wanted to go.

HUNTING WITH MY STEPFATHER
By Shea Thomas & Chris Rensch

My stepdaughter and I (Chris Rensch) went out coon hunting on a cool dark night behind a friends house. We had our best dogs, "Maggie & Money" with us. When we turned them loose they took straight off, not waiting for anything. Within 5 minutes they were treeing. We ended up going to Maggie first. She had the "meat" as we say. We shot the coon out and let her at it. Then we took her to where Money was treeing. He also had the "meat". So I let Shea shoot it out. After we shot it out, we walked up the hill and let them go again. We were walking around this field where we let them go and they had treed again, but this time together. When we got there, there were three coons in the tree. Shea shot the lowest one out and when the dogs were attacking it. One of the other coons ran down the tree and started barking at the dogs. But when Money looked up at it, it ran back up the tree. We both laughed at the coon. We started walking away and the dogs took off and were treeing again. When we got there and looked up, they treed on a 40 foot cliff. Shea ended up falling off a little part of it into the creek. We took the dogs and carefully got to the top and were about to let them go again when Tyler Rensch and Jared Prather showed up. We gave them the dogs, Shea had school the next day and it was time to head home. We ended up with 10 coons that night.

THE ESCAPADES OF GLENN TILLITT AND FAMILY

By Buffy Tillitt-Pratt

While many of these coon hunting stories are told by the actual hunter, I am writing to tell you about my dad, Glenn Tillitt and his coon hunting escapades. Dad died in 1989 and was the greatest coon hunter I knew. To say he loved to coon hunt was an understatement. He hunted coons in Missouri in the early 1900's when he was just a kid, with a lantern and a coon dog that probably slept with him and his brothers. When he moved to Beardstown in the late 40's to start his business he still was devoted to his beloved sport. My memories are best of times when he was over 70 years old and going out night after night much to my moms dismay. He had previously suffered a small stroke, plus had an open heart surgery and other health problems and we were all worried about him being alone in the woods at night. But dad never worried a bit.

When I look back at how he coon hunted, back in the 70's, it was primitive compared to what they have now. There were no cell phones, no gps, and when your dog ran a deer or you got lost you just kept walking in the woods till you found a road, a river, or your truck or someone's house that you could call on a land line to come get ya. You were really in-communicado for the entire hunt. Add to that y mom's worries that he was an old man walking in the woods at night, maybe falling and getting hurt. My mother got more grey hair worrying about dad than about her 3 teenage kids, and for that reason she insisted that dad not hunt alone, but always take a hunting partner. We took our turns going along with him, but the kids had school activities, and mom couldn't go all the time because she felt that both parents shouldn't be out of the house every night. Every night was a requirement for dad during the season, so he had to expand his circle of hunting buddies. Dad liked to teach kids about hunting, and knew two junior high kids, Davey Wells and Little Mike Dyche. They loved to coon hunt as much as he did, plus dad would always let them drive his truck before they got their license, so it was a no brainier that they jumped on the chance to go every time he asked. Dave told me later that dad would say "I want you to practice driving in case I have a heart attack so you can take me to the hospital, If I put 2 nitro glycerin pills under my tongue and am still awake go as fast as you can to the hospital, if I put 3 under my tongue, just drive me to Sager Funeral Parlor!" Sometimes he let the youngsters drive because he couldn't walk good enough through the woods. He had them drive his little Ford truck like it was a tank, telling them to drive through creeks, across ditches, and of course, being young drivers, they often got stuck. Then the pair would walk to a farmer's house at night, and try to borrow a tractor to pull out the little truck. They pulled the bumper off, knocked off the mirrors hitting a tree, and just threw parts in the back and dad fixed it the next day at his Ford Garage. When he would call the boys, and their folks wouldn't let them hunt on a school nights because they had a test the nest day, mom or one of us would go along. I say "had to" but it really was a blessing in later years to remember those nights in the woods with my dad, hearing the dogs bay in the distance. I liked it best when the weather was better, but dad didn't care if it was freezing rain, pelting snow, or below zero. He was going to go coon hunting, and mom didn't like him to be alone. The only time I ever heard him say he wasn't going coon hunting was when there was a full moon. No, he wasn't afraid of vampires, he said the coons wouldn't run because when they came out of the den the light of the moon made them think it was daytime, and they went back in the den to sleep!

There were a few times that dad did go alone, and his dog would run a deer, which always caused problems. Dad would never leave the dog in the woods and call it a night. Coon dogs cost a lot of money, and as I said there was no gps tracking system for them. You didn't want to loose you dog to coyotes, and he would spend all night looking for the dogs, or go back to the truck and wait for him. Sometimes he wouldn't come home till 2 am when the dogs got done running the deer and came back to the truck. One time mom called me about midnight worried because he wasn't home and a blizzard had started. Out we went looking for him, but we didn't know where to look because he hadn't told us where he was hunting that night. We were so worried and couldn't find him, he finally came in about 2:00 am just as we were ready to call the sheriff. He said his dog had run a deer and he waited at the truck and fell asleep. My mom lite into him, saying that if we actually found him, sleeping in his truck, we would have found him and thought he was dead! She screamed "how do you think that would have made me feel to come upon you and think you were dead when you were asleep?" He just smiled and said he couldn't help it because he wouldn't leave his dog in the woods. Those dogs meant the world to him. He loved his coon dogs, and was always on the lookout for the perfect dog. One time a shyster sold him a dog, and promised beyond all that it was the best dog that ever walked the earth. Dad paid a good price for the dog, and all it did was run deer. It never did tree a coon. Dad was mad but couldn't find the guy to make him good on his word, and take the dog back. Well one night Schuyler County Coon Hunters Association was having a night hunt, and low and behold there was the shyster standing by a bonfire. Dad went up to him and started yelling at him, that he was a liar and a crook, and that he wanted his money back on the dog that did nothing but run deer! The guy started laughing at him, and told dad he was gullible. This made dad mad and he shoved him back, and the guy fell down and his glasses fell off and he started yelling, "you hit me, and I am an old man with glasses! I am calling the law!" So the shyster called the sheriff to press charges and when the sheriff came to take a statement, my dad said "No I never hit him, I just pushed him and he fell down, really the only reason I pushed him was to get him far enough away that I could swing on him hard, and at least get a good hit on him, but he fell down first".

Later dad had surgery for an aneurysm at 90 years old, his kidneys failed, and his coon hunting days were few and far between. He took a downturn in the hospital and the doctor called our family all in to say goodbye. We were all standing around him crying, and he said he needed to talk to his son-in-law Jim Ward alone. Everyone thought it had to do with the car dealership, so we left the room thinking that dad was going to give Jim some final advice to help him in the business. But when Jim came out of the hospital room he was laughing and shaking his head. It seemed dad and Ron Gernay had bought a super dooper coon hound on the half's and it was so expensive that mom didn't even know he bought it. Ron was keeping it at his house, and dad was worried that when he died no one would know he paid for half the dog. He wanted Jim to go out to Ron's after he died and tell Ron to pay mom for dad's half, making sure Jim understood, that it was "one hell of a dog". But dad didn't want mom to know that he bought it until after he died because she would kill him if she knew what the dog cost. He was still thinking of his beloved coon dogs just hours before he left this world . . . going to that big coon hunting woods in the sky, where the dogs never run deer, and the trucks never get stuck, and the coons don't come down the trees to fight the dogs. We can look forward to being there some day ourselves.

Until then . . . . Happy coon hunting, my friends.

COON HUNTING WITH DAD

By Richard Utter

Coon hunting was a big part of my dad's life. He preferred coon hunting over other types of hunting, and always said it was his favorite birthday gift, because "coon hunting season" started on November 5th of each year in Illinois, his birthday. I spent a lot of time hunting with dad, Charles Utter Jr. when I was young. Most of the time was spent trying to keep up with him, grasping for a two cell flashlight, following in his footsteps and dodging tree limbs. Most of my pre-teen and early teenage years were spent carrying coon hides and walking a lot. I felt like a pack mule and usually kept up. In those days we hunted usually till about 1:00 or 2:00 am, we would stop at Ford's grocery store for hard candy to take along. Dad usually carried the candy in his coat pocket, and he usually got the ribbon multi colored hard candy.

I do remember the first coon I shot, I think I was 12, and shot him between the eyes with dad's .22 Marlin rifle, he had carried since he was 12. Mom bought him a new .22 rifle one Christmas, but he never used it, stating it was to loud. The old marlin was just heavier and besides I never seen him ever clean the rifle, it has a muffled sound, rather than a crack when he shot it. Over the years he wrapped black electrical tape around the stock and the scope had a crack in the lens, and required at times digging the spent cartridge out with his pocketknife, which was really the only thing that seemed to slow him down. When you shot you had to aim a little to the right to hit what you were shooting. We both thought it was a great shot and I was happy that it only took one shot. One night we were hunting and I talked dad into letting me take the new rifle mom had bought him, while he carried the old marlin. He had called Lloyd Reische of Hersman about going along. All three of us ended up hunting down the Illinois River area near Versailles, down on the bluff, north of the river. We were having a good night and I had asked several times if I could shoot out a coon. Finally, with what seemed to be over half the night, dad said "Ok, the next one is yours, you can shoot it out, just shut up about it." I may have been 13 years old.

I remember it like it was yesterday, the dogs treed on a ridge in a tree on the other side of a deep hollow. Dad said "here is your chance get over here and shoot it out". I remember sliding down the hill into the hollow and crawling up the hill to the other side, making sure not to get the rifle dirty, and excited about my chance. On getting closer to the tree, I ran into a lot of rose bushes, brush, crab apple and thorn trees. It was thick to the point you couldn't walk through it, so I had to crawl under the brush to get to the tree. This seemed to take forever, but I thought I have this chance to shoot this new rifle and its worth it. I finally made it to the tree and was shining my light on the coon, I lifted the rifle, had the coon in my scope sights, and was about to pull the trigger, when I heard a shot from across the hollow. Lloyd carries a pistol in a holster on his belt and was a great shot. He had shot once from where they were, and the coon dropped almost on top of me. It fell right at my feet. I heard Lloyd laughing and saying "thanks Rich for shining your light on the coon for me, it made it easy for me to shoot". They both got a big kick out of it. Dad said "get that coon will ya, since you are closer!" Needless to say I was mad, and they knew it, they both snickered about it the rest of the night. I never got to shoot anything that night, because the dogs never treed anything else. It seemed like a lot of work just to get the coon, and due to the distance a little more light made it easier for Lloyd to shoot. So it was partly my fault. The last comment was "good thing we had you along to crawl under that brush to get that coon, we don't know what we would have done without you". I have to admit I probably would have done the same thing. Besides that, due to the distance, it was an awesome shot with a pistol.

It was probably 1977, dad and I went on the Annual FFA coon hunt. The night was not a good night to hunt, it was warm and the moon was out. Dad said it was going to be tough night to hunt because they were just not going to run that night. He said in order to catch anything we were going to have to find some deep timber. We headed to scab hollow. We hadn't caught anything, the FFA handed out trophies for the biggest coon, the smallest and so on. We ended up in a corn field along a hollow where the dogs had gone. About half way across the field it began to mist, and turned off cloudy, which was good. The dogs hit on a tree down the ridge. Dad said although he hated to, we would have to drop off in a hollow which as he put it "pretty damn deep" "so watch yourself going down and don't get hurt". On getting to the bottom we ended up at the base of the tree, and shot three coons out of a single tree. We weighed each one saving the heaviest for the weigh in. We ended up with eight coons that night out of that hollow. Dad said he hadn't seen that many out of that hollow before that night. All was great and it started to rain, and it came down heavy, water was running down the hill making it nearly impossible to get out of the hollow. I remember this night because it took us both working together to get out of the hollow. We finally made it out and was glad to see the dogs had made it to.

Dad had decided to call it a night, so we cut it short and returned to town soaked through and muddy. Not many coons were caught that night. Two other groups came in behind us. We were almost to late to check in. We ended up with the heaviest coon award that night, but I think we were relieved to be out of that hollow and the rain.

On occasion when dad and I would go hunting, he would call Stan "Steamboat" Kelly to go along. It would really not make a difference what night, or day Stan would go. Stan almost always wore bucked over boots, and they would always come unbuckled and jingle. It was like hunting with Festus from Gunsmoke. At least you knew where he was at all times. Stan seemed to talk non stop about things, nothing in particular, just about everything. Dad never seemed to mind until it came time to listen for the dogs. Getting Stan to shut up for 2 minutes and to stand still was impossible. Dad would say "be quiet Stan, stand still!" That was usually followed by "OOOK Jr" that lasted about 15 seconds, "did you hear anything?" If the dog barked Stan would say "there she is" or "did you hear that?" Dad never got upset with Stan. They had been friends for a long time. Stan worked for dad and my grandfather, Charles "Shorty" Utter on the farm for years, as needed. On a number of occasions we would also take Wilson Murfin along as well. When you got those two together you had quite a pair. Murfin had a medical condition where he shook a lot, and Stan was slow and never shut up. He would talk to Murfin all night and follow us wherever we went. One night we crossed the same fence about five times and they both got turned around so badly neither one knew where we were. This tickled dad because he had gotten them lost on a farm they had both worked on. I just know it was a really good time. Catching coons was important but just having fun was equally important. Having those two made it memorable to me. Equally memorable to me was hunting with Raymond Egbert of Browning. Raymond always seem to carry a carbide light. It had a large dome, in which he kept polishes up to reflect the light. Carbide lights were basically a light which used carbide and water to create a gas, which fed a small flame. The light was useful and was brighter than you may think.. If it worked right. Sometimes through the night, most generally Raymond would stop everything to clean the light by running a little file into the gas port or adding water to the water chamber, or relighting the flame. This light spit all night which to me was very cool/ Dad would sometimes say "Raymond, when are you ever going to get rid of that thing and get yourself a good light, that thing is more trouble than its worth?". I cant write about coon hunting without remembering three dogs which were some of the best dogs we had. All three were walker coon hounds, two males and one female. Duke was the older of the two males and the sire to Boozer the other male, and the female was Kate. Kate was a small soft hearted dog but a good hunter, but she had a terrible habit. If there was a skunk within a mile or smelling distance she would try to kill it. One night we were in Bainbridge Township near Lottie Herren's farm, about to put the dogs in the truck when Kate the last to be loaded, backed off, broke away and looked at dad. She then ran off south towards Irene Hood's house. Dad whistled and yelled for her but she kept going. Dad said "she is going back to kill that skunk we smelled earlier". It didn't take long, we sat in the truck about 15 minutes and waited. I think we smelled her before we saw her. She came back to the truck with her tail between her legs and laid down when dad grabbed her by the collar to put her in the box. She knew she was in trouble. Duke was a dog you could hunt by himself, or with other dogs. Boozer was a fast hard hunting dog. Long legged and fastest of the three he would be out front as he grew older. All three of these dogs were great dogs. Dad trained these dogs well, he would yell "cant get it" and they would pull off the tree, and start running somewhere else. They would beat you to the truck when they heard "lets go home:. They hunted well and knew everything dad would say, and would hunt as long as he wanted. Unfortunately one winter, they all three died from a outbreak of pseudo rabies within a single week. Coon hunting provided us an extra income, money for Christmas, a time to be with friends, a way to control a pest, and plenty of exercise, and in my dad's case a way to really get to know him.

TWO HUNTS

By David Ward

Dick Powell, his sons Rick and Rod, and I took the dogs over to Don Aten's Woodstock farm and started on the former Rodewald farm. The dogs took off and hit a track and started running it. Rod had sat down and had fallen asleep so Dick stayed with him and Rick and I followed the dogs. Larky, the coonhound, had treed a coon. Rick and I went around and around a big old oak tree trying to find the coon but could not because of the leaves. After going around that tree a few times, I got disoriented. For the first time in my life I was lost in the woods. We called out to Dick and when he answered, his voice was not coming from where I thought it should be. Finally we got back to the truck and I knew where we were.

Later that fall, Don Fagan came down from Chicago, where he was training and driving racehorses at the time, and he wanted to go hunting. So Don, Dick Powell, Vick Chockley and I started out. We let the dogs out south of Scripps Park and went down the holler through the Dyson, Scripps and Rodewald ground and over to the Jackson farm where Dick lived at that time. This was a good four hour hunt and found nothing. We had coffee at Dick's house then went back to the car. Fagan said he wanted to see "fur on the tree" before he went back to Chicago that night so we headed out again and the car ran out of gas. We started pushing the car up to Ping's Pantry for gas and decided that was not going to work. So I walked up to Ping's. Beulah Ham was working and I borrowed her car and drove to dad's house, got a gas can and went back to the guys.

After we dropped off Beulah's car, I told the guys to take me home I had to get up early for work. They went out again and finally treed a coon. Don got to see "fur on the tree" that night.

A HUNT I WILL NEVER FORGET

By Kenneth Wenger

The year was 2005 and I was a member of the Schuyler County Coon Hunters Association. On the night of September 3rd, the club had a youth hunt. We had a total of seven youth hunt that night. Ron Beaird, Justin Dupoy, and Kerry Hoover. I guided the youngest boys consisting of Kidd Baker and his dad Kenny, Tristan Dupoy and his dad Pete, and Braden Forsythe and his dad Joe. We all met at the clubhouse at the fairgrounds and enjoyed a meal before the hunt. You could see the excitement building in the boys' eyes and in their voices. On this night they were going to be handling their own dogs on the hunt. The sky's finally got dark and we loaded the dogs and the boys and headed out to one of my farms where one of my most memorable hunts was about to start. The farm had a little stream of water flowing through the center of it. We crossed the stream and parked beside a standing cornfield. The dads helped the boys get their dogs on their leashes and get ready to cast them off on their hunt. The cast of dogs was represented by three different breeds: Kidd Baker's dog was a blue tick named Boss, Tristan Dupoy was hunting a English female named Anne, and last but not least, Braden Forsythe was hunting a Redbone male named Rowdy. The boys cast their dogs off and into the cornfield the dogs went with the boys behind them. It did not take very long for the boys to come running back out of the cornfield. Kidd Baker's pup was probably 3 months old, so he did not hunt to far, which was fine with the boys, they had a pup to play with. I can remember standing there with all the lights off but the ones the boys had, listening to them play. It was a perfect night for coon hunting. It was cool with a slight breeze blowing the standing corn. I'll never forget the boys kept getting a little braver and a little braver when they finally decided to go into the cornfield by themselves. One of the boys said to the other "stop!, did you hear that?" Here they came running out of the cornfield. In no time at all they all headed back into the cornfield not knowing what was about to happen. I waited until they stopped and then I threw an ear of corn out into the field. You could hear that ear go through the different rows of corn on its descent to the ground. This is when the boys got excited. They were screaming "what was that?" and here they came. Now if you have ever been out in a cornfield at dark and the corn is about 10 feet tall, you might know how hard it is to get back out of the cornfield through the rows running crossways, not to mention not knowing what was out there with you. It sounded like a group of calves running in the cornfield. The boys finally make it out of the field and came over and stood by the adults and asked if we heard anything. Some of the boys wanted to go back in the cornfield, but one of them was not sure about that. After a little persuasion from the other two, they started back into the cornfield. We could hear them say "stop" and ask "do you hear anything yet?" Not hearing they proceeded into the field even farther. Once again I threw an ear of corn again followed by another and another. That was enough. The young hunters were making ground up fast, coming at us as fast as their little legs would carry them. We all had a good laugh with them, and in all the fun the dogs had treed on the other side of the cornfield. It took us a little while to get to where the dogs were. We helped the boys put the dogs on their leads and began to shine the tree looking for the coon. The boys were so happy when someone said "there he is". We headed back to the trucks and loaded the boys and coon dogs up. We went back to the clubhouse where each boy was given a plaque for the nights hunt. A good time was had by all. It definitely was the best hunt I have ever been on. Thanks Kidd, Tristan, Braden for the hunt of a lifetime.

OL SMOKE

By Mike Wise

I was glad when Don asked me to write a little story for his book. It meant a lot to me that he see's me as a "coon hunter". I met a lot of good people and hunted with a lot of good hunters in the years I followed the hounds through the woods. I still today, wish things were like they once were when you could free cast a hound on almost on anyone's property. In this day and age you can't so it like we once did with all the property leases' and outfitters out there for deer and turkey hunting. This is one of the reasons I do not hunt anymore and I sure do miss it. I have had the pleasure to have followed 3 or 4 pretty good dogs in my life but one stands out to me as the best. He was an English Blue male and I called him Smoke. He was a natural from the first time I saw him. A good friend of mine Ron Beaird told me about this young blue dog that Chip Anderson, from Ellisville had for sale. So we went to try him out one night and this little dog split treed from his mother that night on a den tree. He was a mere 6 ½ months old. when I bought him under that den tree! I hunted the hair off that dog and loved every night we turned him loose. Some were good some not, but that's coon hunting. You really don't know how good a dog is until they are gone, but I have many memories of that dog and one in particular stands out.

It was a very cold and very damp night in late January and I hunted almost every night of the season. Ol Smoke was as tired as I was but when it's in your blood you go anyway. We went that night to Industry, IL to a friends I had met at our local coon hunters club. Dave Lancaster and his boy's Andrew and Phillip loved to hunt. They asked me to come up around 6:00 pm and we hit the woods. Andrew had a little Blue English female named "Lady" and I had Smoke. We hunted for four hours or so and we treed three coons. We took a little break for about an hour and had birthday cake and coffee. Well, Andrew and I were hard pressed to get Dave back out but we finally got him to go with us. We hunted until about midnight and only in den trees. It was one of those nights when the frost had fell so heavy late in the night that it looked like it had snowed. Dave said he was ready to call it a night, but I was not satisfied, I needed one more chance to tree one on the outside. Dave said there was not a dog around that could tree a coon on the outside on a night like this. That was all it took for me to try to prove him wrong. I got Ol Smoke out of the box and we cut him loose down this holler towards Dave's house. He was gone 15-20 minutes and we hadn't heard a peep out of him. Dave said "well you better get your tracker out to see where he was". When I started to get my receiver out of the truck I heard him open up down the holler. I think it was about an hour total time from the time he opened the first time till the time he treed. He only barked four times on the whole track and then that big bawl locate and I knew when it was over. We made a friendly wager of a piece of birthday cake if we had him on the outside. When we walked to the tree I had my doubts that we would see him. I turned on my spotlight and backed away from this huge oak tree there he was sitting in the first fork right over the top of a huge hole in the tree. Me not being the best shot and not wanting him to get away, I pulled up and aimed right at his left ear. I couldn't believe I knocked him out on the first shot. That old ringtail was so big we took him to the house un skinned to weigh him. 28 ½ lbs, one of the biggest coons Ol Smoke had ever treed. I asked Dave what he thought about my old dog now. He laughed and said "if I hadn't seen it I wouldn't have believed it". I think that night made me realize what kind of dog I really had. I hunted several good dogs after that but none as good as Ol Smoke. By the way that cake was pretty good too!

MY FIRST HUNT

By Donald Young

My first hunt was when I was about six years old. I went with my dad John Paul and Wayne Morrell. My grandfather fixed me up with an old kerosene lantern, dad had a flashlight and Wayne had a carbide light. Off we went around a cornfield and soon the dogs opened up. Dad and Wayne took off running and I tried to keep up, but before long they left me behind. I turned up the wick in the lantern for more light. Wrong! The globe sueted up inside and I couldn't see three feet in front of me. It became dark and I got lost. I couldn't hear the dogs or dad. I just stopped in the cornfield, then I heard shots. Later here came the dogs, dad, Wayne and their coon. They took me back to the truck and went back out to hunt. Boy was I scared when they left me and I couldn't see. It was probably a good thing I stayed in the truck because they would have likely had me pack those dead coons around. When they returned I got to watch Wayne skin out those coons. . . . . . Yuck!

LEAVE THE WHISKEY AT HOME WHEN YOU COON HUNT

By Donald Young

One night I took Dave Kilpatrick hunting with me while his two kids were with their grandfather Bill Bartlett. Dave jumped into my truck and off we went south of the Sargent home. Well Dave forgot his flashlight, but out came a bottle of Jack Daniels. OH NO! We were out hunting for a couple of hours and Dave with no light. He stayed right on my butt. Every once in a while I held on to a tree limb and then let it go and gave Dave a good swat. We tree a coon in a big old white oak tree. I told Dave if you help me get to that first limb, I think I can get to the den hole. I looked down the hole, nothing, but when I looked up I could see coon tails. I took out my pistol and with one shot out one came, with the second shot, down it went and Rasstus, my dog took care of it. I saw another coon in the hole. I did the same and down it went. Again I found the third one and again I did the same thing. Three jumbo coons! I couldn't believe it. So the fun really started when I tried to get down, it was sure easier to get up than down. Boy, I was sure glad to hit the ground safely. Well, we started to pack the coons back to the truck. The heavier they got the more breaks we took and the emptier the booze bottle became. Besides that, we were celebrating our hunt. I'm not much of a drinker but Dave twisted my arm and forced me to help him finish the Jack Daniels!! Those coons just kept getting heavier so I decided to skin them out. The first big tree with a low branch was where we stopped. I had some binder twine in my pocket and extra pocket knives. So we lined up two coons, and used my wheat light to shine on both coons. While we were skinning we started cutting and pulling and we kept the limb bouncing, when we finished skinning the coons we were all cut up, plus the coons too!. I always carried a few bandages, but not nearly enough. When we got home we needed more first aid. The next day I took those three coons into town to the fur buyer. He just laughed and told me to take them back home and learn how to dress out a coon, those were ruined. It took a couple of weeks for our hands to heal from all the cuts. Leave the booze along when you go coon hunting!

RASSTUS

By Donald Young

I started coon hunting on my own just after I got married in 1973. My father-in-law got me a Tennessee Cur, Plot dog, walnut in color, with a stub tail. I called him Rasstus. I bought me a carbide light and was in business. The dog was trained fairly well. My father-in-law came several times to help me, and to show me how to skin the coons and to take care of the hides. I went many times with the neighbor boy. He had a dog that liked to tree possums and it just about ruined my dog.

We had an old church down the road that the Coon Hunters Club had bought for a club house.

Every month we had a weigh in with prizes for the heaviest coon. They served fried fish, hotdogs, sometimes chili and gallons of coffee. Oh the stories they would tell and some of the outfits they wore. They range from fine hunting coats to rags like mine. I've heard stories about some guys putting an old window weight inside the coons so it weighed more.

I came close to getting me a riding mule to hunt on. Dick Powell, Don Fagan, Ronnie Hess and John Rutledge just about talked me into one, but those boys didn't know when to go home at night, and I had to work the next morning, so I backed out. When you are hunting in the woods and it starts snowing, things change, I almost got lost in my own woods.

PICK AND SHOOT

By Donald Young

I had the FFA kids at school make me a dog box with two compartments. I hunted with several hunters, one was Gerald Curry and his walker dog. I still had Rasstus, the Plot dog. The first night we treed eight coons in one large oak tree. It looked like a Christmas tree lit up. Gerry said he had seen this before, and for us to pick out a coon, but not the same one, then count together, then on three shoot at the same time. He said they will all jump out of the tree at the same time. So, we shot two out, and sure enough they all fell like you shook the limb and ran in different directions. They all disappeared, I never saw the likes before. Some of them must have jumped 15-20 feet out of that tree and they were gone that fast. Gerry and I hunted about three more times and each time our dogs would get into bad fights. I thought that it was my dog that started the fights since he was a Tennessee Cur, and they are known for being a fighting dog. So I took Rasstus back to my father-in-law. Later Gerry said he hunted with someone else and his dog got into another fight. So I guess we got rid of the wrong dog.

AMOS AND ALMA
By Donald Young

When coon prices were around $30.00 dollars Bill Crum and I decided to go into the business of coon hunting. Bill and I bought a pair of young registered Blue Tick male pups, brothers from Breeze Mitchell's female. I named my dog Amos Moses. I don't know if we trained the dogs or if they trained us, but we had fun. They followed us more than we followed them. They had trouble getting over, around and under fences. We just kept walking away from them, we left them crying and then in a while here they would come. After we got the first coon and made sure it was good and dead they got to play tug of war and wrestle with it for long time. We never let the coon get the best of the dogs. As long as the dogs got the upper hand on the coons they thought they were top dogs. Each hunt it got easier for them. On several occasions a possum, rabbit or a deer would lead them off course, a few spankings and a few choice words took care of that. I think they chased a squirrel if they were out late that night. Those dogs were sure a lot of fun. Once I took Bill back home from a hunt, let his dog out and forgot to turn off my wheat light. I got into my frost covered truck and backed over his mailbox.

Later Bill got discouraged with his dog and sold him. I bought a female Blue tick from Ronnie Hess and named her Alma Lou. Amos and Alma, don't you think that sounds like a good pair? Poor Alma got car sick in her dog box every time we went out. She never did get over that. Later in years Amos got a sore on his elbow, it got so bad the vet thought it was cancer and he would have to amputate. I pondered about this. He died two weeks later. Alma was in the pen next to where Amos was and died about two weeks after Amos, the vet said she died from loneliness, because they had always been together. Man . . . I was out of business quickly, then my wheat lite fizzled out and you can not buy carbide anywhere. I really was out of business! The coon prices had dropped to $5.00-$10.00 dollars. It didn't hardly pay for vet shots and dog feed. Now the coon hunting woods are mostly leased out to outfitters and deer hunters and no trespassing signs are everywhere. A person can't hardly find a place to hunt, and the dogs sure don't know where the boundary lines are. About the only thing I got left from my coon hunting days is an old chewed up dog box and memories. The dog kennel is now a chicken pen! We have 7 hens and 1 rooster. FRESH EGGS! they taste better than coons anyway!

FFA 2012

By Donald Young

I no longer hunt but I have supported the annual FFA "Buddy Coon Hunt" for several years. I liked watching the younger generation bring in their coons to be weighed at midnight. It's hard for me to stay up that late, but It's worth it. The hunters turned in 130 coons last January 2010. The FFA has a prize of $300.00 dollars for the heaviest, then the most and a lucky weight number. They sell raffle tickets for donated prizes. They have lots of food and drinks for the hungry hunters. It sure does bring back fond memories of good old days of coon hunting.